Judith Gautier

Richard Wagner and his Poetical Work

Judith Gautier

Richard Wagner and his Poetical Work

ISBN/EAN: 9783337306991

Printed in Europe, USA, Canada, Australia, Japan

Cover: Foto ©Thomas Meinert / pixelio.de

More available books at **www.hansebooks.com**

RICHARD WAGNER

AND

His Poetical Work

FROM

"RIENZI" TO "PARSIFAL"

BY

JUDITH GAUTIER

TRANSLATED WITH THE AUTHOR'S SPECIAL
PERMISSION

By L. S. J.

BOSTON

A. WILLIAMS AND COMPANY

Old Corner Bookstore

1883

ELECTROTYPED.

BOSTON STEREOTYPE FOUNDRY,
NO. 4 PEARL STREET.

AMERICAN INTRODUCTION.

RICHARD WAGNER was born May 22, 1813, in
Leipsic, Germany. He died in Venice on February
13, 1883. His father was a Leipsic city official, who
gave his son the benefit of the illustrious Thomas
School, preparatory to a university career. The lat-
ter, however, was not of much advantage to him, as
young Wagner devoted himself mainly to musical
studies. He led a theatre orchestra in Magdeburg,
then in Königsberg, then in Riga.

From the latter place he went, in 1839, to Paris,
where he completed " Rienzi " and the " Flying
Dutchman," in 1841. The latter was suggested by
a gale which Wagner experienced during a short
voyage. " Rienzi " was first brought out at Dres-
den in 1842, and led to Wagner's appointment as
orchestra leader in Dresden, where he brought out
his " Tanhäuser " in 1845. In 1849 Wagner had to
leave Germany for political reasons, and went to
Switzerland, where " Lohengrin " was finished and
the tetralogy of the " Nibelung " was begun. Wag-
ner then lived in Italy, Vienna, and Paris, where
" Tanhäuser " met with a disastrous presentation in
1861, and led accidentally to the following pages.

3

In 1864 Wagner became intimate with Louis II.,
the young King of Bavaria, under whose zealous
patronage he brought out his "Tristan" ·   - -
the "Mastersingers" in 1768, " Rhinegold
the "Walkyria " in 1870, — all at Munich.
wrote the text for his operas, and also numerous
pamphlets, most of which led to acrimonious dis-
cussions. Wagner's musical ideals received some
outward impulses from the Oberammergau passion
play,•and the success of the Franco-Prussian war,
which led to the establishment of the German Em-
pire. A special Wagner theatre was begun in 1872
at Bayreuth, where the master has since lived, and
his works were first presented in 1876, in entire
harmony with his vast requirements. Wagner's last
work, "Parsifal," was published in 1878.

Wagner's early writings were collected in an edi-
tion of nine volumes, published in Leipsic, 1871 to
1873. His life was written by Glasenapp in two
volumes, 1876 to 1878. Kastner published a Wag-
ner catalogue. But it will take years, perhaps dec-
ades, before a final and just estimate can be formed
of so great a master. The following pages were
written by Judith Gautier, the Paris writer, and trans-
lated by an American lady. They have gone through
several European editions, as they give an account
of Wagner's opera texts,· and pay a tribute to the
genius of the great composer, who was also a remark-
able and original author.

PREFACE

WILL the reader kindly look upon the first pages of this book as a fragment of reminiscences, which I hope some day to publish ; not that my life in itself is worth relating, but it has been frequently brought in contact with that of celebrated artists. It treats here of certain experiences only, written as if for myself, — reminiscences gathered during several years of uninterrupted relations with Richard Wagner. The books already published on the master, in every language and every style, either to combat or glorify him, would fill a shelf ; the catalogue of these criticisms, studies, and biographies would form a volume. Thus, the subject of his defeats, victories, and what is termed his musical system, has been exhausted ; repetition is therefore useless.

Beside this, I have of late renounced all idea of proselytism ; after a long struggle I abandon the contest, at the moment when, to many, victory seems most probable. I have reasons for this which I do not care to indicate, but which seem to me decisive. What I have for so long a time taken to be the customary and fatal resistance, the instinctive hatred which is experienced by every public in every country for the innovations of genius, is, I fear, in France something even more. Our quick intelligence, so light, so mobile, so disposed to mockery, deprives us of that quality so indispensable to the comprehension of master works — simplicity. We cannot refrain from finding something to ridicule in grand sentiments, sublimity, and noble or terrible passions; what pleases us above all is graceful, spirited art, slightly sentimental, quick observation, and arrows of satire; also, no people can rival us when comic operas, vaudevilles, and comedies of manners are in question.

Art is for us an amusement. We frankly weary of anything serious, and if by chance we happen to admit a masterpiece upon the scenes, it is simply on the score of curiosity. Does a theatre exist in Paris, this world's capital, where the great works, lyrical and dramatic, of the entire world may be represented? Who troubles himself about Calderon, Schiller, Goethe, Shakspeare? While absurd fairy scenes and miserable comedies, in which the only discoverable merit is the play or personality of the actors, and scenes of disgraceful realism, remain upon the boards during a whole year, Othello drags painfully on, barely reaching the twentieth representation. It will, perhaps, be urged that the Frenchman dare not travel, and that works of art created outside of his own little world do not interest him. And Victor Hugo! Is there any sort of indignity or outrage which has been spared him in his own country ? It is true, that after sixty years of contest, his glory radiates at last splendid and triumphant. Well, where is Victor Hugo's theatre ? Has the new generation ever seen the representations of this master's greatest works? "Les Burgraves," "Cromwell," and "Le Roi qui S'Amuse." This last drama, it is true, is about to reappear upon the stage. But fifty years will have intervened between its first and second representations. Why hope that Richard Wagner should stand a better chance of vanquishing the native antipathy of the French public to serious works than Shakspeare, who after three hundred years has not yet triumphed among us ; than Victor Hugo, the greatest glory of France ? Are the enchantments of music capable of working this miracle ? It is possible, but I no longer hope for it. The success of Lohengrin in Paris is probable, but we shall go no farther. Neither the great Scandinavian epopée, nor the metaphysical loves of Tristan and Isolde, nor the mysticism of Parsifal will reach us. For this reason, recognizing the generous error in which I have so long persisted, I renounce all sterile efforts, and, blessing the invention of railroads, I go bravely toward the mountain which cannot be brought to me.

This book is, in reality, only addressed to the small number of the initiated who, having broken through the occult precinct of the new art, have the incomparable joy of admiring without reserve all that is worthy of admiration. They will find in these pages, in addition to certain characteristic traits of the master, drawn from life, and from which they will be able to modify the ideas which they may have received from fantastic portraits, the detailed analyses of poems which have not been translated into French, and, above all, that of Parsifal. These analyses will enable those undertaking the pilgrimage to Bayreuth, and who do not understand German, to follow the representations. My sole ambition is to be useful to the extent of my power to this intelligent minority, who, in my opinion, alone form this world, and who, I truly hope, may alone form another, should it exist; for I am convinced, with Charles Baudelaire, that paradise is made up of the small number of chosen ones.

CONTENTS.

RICHARD WAGNER.

RICHARD WAGNER.

It was under rather peculiar circumstances that the name of Wagner was mentioned in my presence, for the first time, the evening of the first representation of Tanhäuser in Paris. I had left school the day before on a vacation, and if this great combat in regard to Tanhäuser had been mentioned in my hearing, I, at least, remembered nothing of it. I was accidentally crossing the Passage de l'Opéra with my father, the evening of this representation, during an *entr'acte*. The passage was crowded ; a gentleman, who approached my father with a bow, stopped us. He was rather small, thin, with hollow cheeks and a prominent nose, a broad forehead and brilliant eyes. He

13

began to speak of the representation, at which he had been present, with malignant intensity, and such a ferocious joy at seeing the confirmation of its failure, that, carried away by an involuntary sentiment, I suddenly emerged from the silence and reserve imposed upon one of my age, to cry with astonishing impertinence, " In hearing you, sir, it is easy to divine that a great work is in question, and that you speak of a brother-artist."

" Now, what has come over you, naughty child," said my father, wishing to reprove me, but quietly laughing to himself. " Who is it?" I asked, when the gentleman had left us. " That was Hector Berlioz."

I have never forgotten this incident, and I have seemed later to see in this sudden movement of anger, which roused my young conscience to indignation in so singular a manner, a sort of presentiment, — something which premonished me that one day I should become a passionate admirer of this artist, whose name I now heard for the first time.

It seems evident that, at the moment when a new genius reveals itself, a little group of chosen mortals springs to life, called to form about him a devoted company to defend him, to console him for all but universal hatred, to sustain him in his agonies, all the while upholding the divinity of his inspirations. It was doubtless my vocation to become a disciple of this new hero, to understand and believe in him, for I was influenced by no one. One day chance placed in my hands the score of the Flying Dutchman. My music teacher, who hired music at Flaxland's, had taken this volume, among others, without knowing its contents, and left it with me until the next lesson, as it was inconveniently burdensome. I had profited little by my lessons, and was a most indifferent pianist; notwithstanding which, after having deciphered in the most incomplete and crude manner this unknown score, I was entirely overcome, and in spite of my numberless mistakes, the grandeur and meaning of this music were revealed to me by a sort of intuition. I could not be persuaded to leave the piano; I became infatuated, and my friends tried in vain to get the score out of my hands. From this moment Richard Wagner had one more faithful disciple.

When, in 1868, I wrote several articles upon his works, I had still a very imperfect knowledge of them from more or less satisfactory executions upon the piano and desultory fragments heard at the popular concerts. I was much alarmed at my own audacity, after having addressed these articles to Wagner, then at Lucerne, accompanied by a letter, begging him to aid me kindly with his advice for their correction and completion. I hoped and waited for an answer with extreme anx-

iety: would it come? I could not believe
it, and yet I could think of nothing else.
I could hardly sleep, and as each morning
passed, and the messenger brought nothing,
my heart filled with anguish. One day,
however, I spied the Lucerne postmark
upon an envelope addressed in an un-
known hand, which I immediately recog-
nized as remarkable.

I held this letter a long time between
my fingers before opening it. I experi-
enced a strange emotion, — a sort of fear.
How had I dared, with my heedlessness,
characteristically French, to write, con-
fiding alone in my instinct, upon the
works of this artist, for whom I felt
already such an enthusiasm that I could
only imagine him as existing, after the
manner of the gods, upon an inaccessible
Olympus. Was this letter really from
him? I opened it at last, four pages of
elegant handwriting, very legible, and at
the last line the magic signature. The

letter began thus: "Madam, — It is impossible that you could have experienced the slightest doubt of the touching and kindly impression made upon me by your letter and your fine articles. Accept my thanks for them, and permit me to count you among the small number of true friends whose clear-eyed sympathy is my only glory. There is nothing in your articles to correct, nothing to suggest; but I perceive that you have not yet a thorough knowledge of the Mastersingers." He then gave me an interesting explanation of the introduction to the third act in the Mastersingers, which had been performed by Pasdeloup a short time previous at the popular concerts. The letter ended thus: —

"Pardon me, madam, if I venture to complete, above all with the aid of my bad French, your acquaintance, otherwise so profound and intimate, with my music, by which you have truly touched and sur-

prised me. I shall probably visit Paris
before long, perhaps even this winter, and
I rejoice beforehand in the true pleasure of
taking you by the hand, and telling you
face to face of the pleasure you have given
to your truly obliged and devoted,

RICHARD WAGNER."

I waited in vain for this proposed
journey. Wagner did not visit France
during that winter. Nor has he come
since then. There was but one thing to
be done, — go to Lucerne. But how
should I be received? Fantastic legends
were reported in regard to Wagner;
among others, it was related that he had
in his house a seraglio, composed of
women of all colors, from all countries, in
magnificent costumes; but that no visitor
crossed the threshold of his dwelling.
On the other hand, persons who pre-
tended to know him intimately, depicted
him as an unsocial man, gloomy and sul-

len, living in jealous retreat, having for
sole companionship two large black dogs.
This wild solitude was tolerable, and even
pleased me; but the idea that a feeling of
polite gratitude might force him to break
through it in my favor troubled me
greatly. On this account I wrote an ex-
tremely complicated letter, saying, that
passing through Lucerne by chance, only
passing, I begged him to inform me if he
were still there and would permit me the
pleasure of greeting him. By this arrange-
ment the fear of his disturbance being
prolonged beyond that of a short interview
would be averted. To tell the truth,
chance had nothing to do with this journey,
and there was nothing to hurry me. The
following letter · entirely reassured me:
" Madam, — I am at Lucerne, and I have
no need to tell you how much pleasure
I shall have in seeing you. I shall but
beg you to prolong your sojourn at
Lucerne in order that the happiness you

accord me may not vanish too quickly. I suppose that you go to Munich for the exposition of pictures; however, as I have the presumption to believe that it will be agreeable to you to hear some of my works, I would inform you that the representation of Tanhäuser, Lohengrin, Tristan, and the Mastersingers will take place in the month of June, that the theatre is at the present moment closed, and that Rhinegold will be given at the earliest on the 29th of August, if indeed it be given then. But I trust that neither the postponement of the exposition, nor the closing of the theatre, will retard your visit to Lucerne. Quite on the contrary, I shall hope for a prolongation of your stay here, and while begging you to kindly notify me by a word, of the day when you expect to arrive, I pray you to accept the assurance of my respectful gratitude.

RICHARD WAGNER."

I arrived in Lucerne on a beautiful afternoon in the month of July, 1869. On entering the station I looked out of the carriage-door, when I suddenly perceived Wagner on the platform. He did not in the least resemble the unfavorable photographs which I had seen. I had no hesitation in recognizing him and ran toward him. We shook hands in silence, and he enveloped me with that intense glance which is peculiar to himself, and seems to pierce one's soul. I experienced no embarrassment during that moment of strange silence, in which my heart was, so to speak, bare beneath his gaze, but a profound emotion, a wild joy. " Come," he said, offering me his arm, "If you do not care for magnificence, the Lake Hotel will please you; I have engaged rooms there." The hotel was near by, and we went on foot. He stopped a moment on the way, and with a very grave, almost solemn expression, said to me: "We are bound

by a very noble sentiment, madam." But
an instant later, after having recom-
mended me to the innkeeper, he took
leave of me. " I am going to prepare for
your reception," he said, " else I should
be stupid. Come presently when you have
taken a little rest." From my window I
saw him move away with a rapid step,
cross the old bridge of Lucerne, and step
into a boat. He told me later that he
was in haste to impart to his wife his
impressions, which were not in the least
what he had anticipated. At sunset I
reached Tribscheu, that consecrated bit of
land where, since that time, I have passed
so many charming hours.

It was a sort of promontory, extremely
picturesque, jutting into the lake. There
was neither grating nor door; the garden
had no defined limits, and extended indefi-
nitely toward the neighboring mountains.
The exterior of the house was perfectly
plain, — gray, with dark tiles; but in the

interior arrangements, full of grace and
elegance, one felt the presence of a
woman. Madame Wagner appeared in
the midst of her children, fair, tall and
gracious, with a charming smile, and
tender, dreamy-blue eyes. The sympathy
with which she inspired me from the first
moment has never been broken, and our
friendship, already of long standing, has
never known a cloud. It was a delightful
evening; the master displayed incom-
parable animation and gayety of spirits. I
was unprepared for this vivacity of mind,
these witticisms, the delicacies of lan-
guage which we are wont to consider the
monopoly of the Parisian, and .which ac-
quired in him a peculiar charm from his
foreign accent, and, in spite of the great
facility with which he spoke French, his
original and unexpected expressions. He
spoke of Paris, where he had greatly suf-
fered, but which he still loved, and of the
great contest over Tanhäuser, without

bitterness. I remember, among others, this phrase: "Since the public at the opera do not like my music why inflict it upon them?" The group of warm partisans which had formed itself in France appeared to touch him deeply. Perhaps he founded secret hopes upon the initiative spirit of the French. In spite of his steadily increasing success in Germany he still had bitter adversaries, and was still exposed to base persecutions. The press reviled him incessantly with a coarseness and violence of which our French journals, even those most eager for scandal, can give no idea. The calumnies went even so far that Wagner, for the first and last time in his life, decided to reply to them. "I have seen," he said, among other things, "the London and Paris papers mock my works and tendencies without pity; these works have been dragged through the mire, they have been hissed in the theatres; but it still remained to me to see my person, my private character, my domestic life, exposed to public contempt in the country where my works are admired, and where a masculine energy and lofty aspirations are recognized in my efforts." The nobility and clergy were arrayed against him. What they sought for in him was doubtless the revolutionist of the days in May, 1849; the deep thinker, the powerful and energetic man of action, marching toward progress and the liberation of thought. And what hatred! Banished, pursued, and not knowing where to take refuge. Thus came about this almost incredible thing, that, at one time, he might be thought the only German who had not seen the representation of Lohengrin.

Notwithstanding the unalterable affection of King Louis II. he was, at the time I saw him, morally exiled from Bavaria. His long-cherished project of a theatre, the plans of which were already drawn by the great architect, Semper, and which the king wished to have erected in Munich, nearly revolutionized the city. The project was relinquished and the plaster model of the building was sorrowfully banished to an attic in the palace. But Wagner had not ceased to think of it, and who knows if at this moment Paris was not the aim of his dreams? He was then working upon the third part of the Nibelungen, Siegfried. I saw the manuscript on his study piano, in a little apartment adjoining the drawing-room. There was a portrait of his noble friend, handsome as a hero of the Edda. I was told that he sometimes escaped from Munich to pass a few days at Tribscheu, and that in this same room a bed was arranged for him.

There is nothing more touching than the enthusiastic affection with which this young king was inspired by the man of

genius.   He came to him like a saving
angel at the moment when all abandoned
him.   " What shall I say to you," wrote
Wagner to a friend, some time after his
first interview with the king; "the most
incomprehensible thing, and the only one,
moreover, which could save me, is com-
pletely realized.   In the very year of my
first representation of Tanhäuser, a queen
brought into this world the good genius of
my life, him who was destined later, in
the depth of my distress, to give me safety
and consolation.   It seems as if he had
been sent me from heaven."   The king
was obliged, however, to do battle for his
great friend, for the entire court was hos-
tile to him, and the struggle was not with-
out danger for the newly-crowned youth.
But nothing could change his heart.   The
world in general revenged itself upon him
by inventing various legends more or less
absurd and unworthy of his notice.   His
only peculiarity lies in his deep intelli-

gence, and his preference for masterpieces over the frivolous and commonplace pleasures of the world.

For fifteen days I passed my afternoons and evenings in the charming retreat Tribscheu, for I soon had the honor of being considered a friend. When minds are once in sympathy hearts come quicker to an understanding, and my affection for my host soon equalled the admiration with which the artist had inspired me. Of all the information given me about Wagner, his home life, the great reality, was the one black spot. Rus was a handsome Newfoundland, very gentle and pacific, who often came by himself to see me at the Lake Hotel. Few visitors ever crossed the threshold of the master's house. He knew no one at Lucerne, and this tranquillity was favorable to his work. Thus I saw him alone with his family, in all the simplicity of his life, and could form an exact idea of his character. I was greatly struck in the first place by his powerful, resolute head, the extraordinary brilliancy of his eyes, and his intensity of expression. There was also an expression of infinite goodness, which would never be suspected from his portraits. This almost superhuman goodness radiated from him at every moment; it was visible in the adoration with which he inspired not only his family but all who surrounded him. The members of his little domain took advantage of this gentleness. Little by little relations of every degree, near or far, gathered about him, who having come for a visit stayed indefinitely. As I knew the master better, I gained a further insight into his exquisite tenderness of soul, which in him has nothing in common with the vulgar philanthropy so frequently met with, and which is for the most part theoretic. It was a Frenchman, the Count of Gobineau, who said of Wagner, "He can never be absolutely happy, for he will always have some one near him whose sorrows he feels bound to share."

One day I asked him if he had any plans for his new-born son. "My first ambition," he said, "is to assure him a modest income, which will render him independent, that he may be sheltered from the miserable annoyances from which I have so cruelly suffered. Then I should wish him to know something of surgery, enough to render aid to a wounded person in emergencies, to prepare a first dressing. I have so often been troubled by my own inability that I wish to spare him this pain. Beyond this I shall leave him entirely free." Madame Wagner told me that the composition of the Mastersingers had been suspended during long months on account of a sick dog, wandering and abandoned, which Wagner, then at Zurich, had picked up and endeavored to cure. The dog had bitten his right hand badly, and the wound became so painful as to prevent him from writing. It is impossible to dictate music, and he was thus reduced to inaction, which put his patience to a hard test; but the dog was none the less cared for. There are, however, violence and roughness in Richard Wagner's character which must be recognized, and which are frequently the cause of his being misjudged, but only by those who regard merely the exterior. Nervous and impassionable to excess, the emotions which he experiences are always carried to an extreme. With him slight pain is almost despair, the smallest irritation has the appearance of madness. This wonderful organization of such exquisite sensibility has terrible vibrations, and his resistance of them is wonderful. A day of anxiety ages him ten years, but, happiness once reinstated, the day following finds him younger than ever. He gives himself to others with extraordinary prodigality. Always sincere, his whole heart is in everything he does; but of an ex-

tremely variable temper, his opinions and
ideas, fixed the first moment, are by no
means irrevocable. No one recognizes an
error more quickly than he does, but he
must have passed his first enthusiasm. By
his frankness and vehemence he often
wounds his best friends unintentionally;
always excessive he goes farther than he
intends, and does not recognize the grief
he causes. Many, wounded in their self-
love, bear in silence the injury which ag-
gravates them, and thus they lose a precious
friendship; whereas, if they had cried out
that they were hurt, they would have found
the master filled with such sincere regrets
that he would have made an effusive effort
to console them, and their love for him
would only have increased.

"With Wagner the second movement
is the good one," said a French violinist,
who had left everything to enroll him-
self in the orchestra at Bayreuth, — an
artist of great merit, a man of spirit,

who was one of those preferred by
the master. In spite of his occasion-
ally rough manner, Wagner is, when he
so chooses, a perfect charmer. There
is nothing to be compared with the
fascination which he exercises upon the
interpreters working under his orders.
After a few days the most hostile and
rebellious orchestra becomes attached
to him. It is the same with the singers,
whom he inspires with unbounded devo-
tion. The illustrious Schnorr, the first
singer of Tristan, in which part he was
sublime, cried, as he drew his last breath,
" It is not I then who will sing Siegfried."
He regretted nothing in this life but the
glory of interpreting Wagner's works.
One of the most remarkable things about
Wagner is the youthful gayety which so
frequently breaks out, and the charming
good humor which his tormented life has
never been able to quench. His entertain-
ing and profound conversation will

become all at once, without transition, full of humor and imagination. He tells stories in the most comical manner, with a fine irony which belongs to him alone. At Lucerne he surprised me by his skill in bodily exercises, and by his singular agility. He climbed the highest trees in his garden, to the terror of his wife, who besought me not to look at him, because, she said, if he were encouraged he would commit no end of follies.

He was then working very regularly, rising early in the morning. At midday he was free, took long walks, or rested while reading, for he has an insatiable thirst for literature, and is an indefatigable student. In these hours of rest and meditation he has moments of beautiful serenity. His features then assume an incomparable sweetness, his face becomes enveloped with a pallor which has nothing of ill-health, but seems to veil it with a slight cloud. At these moments nothing

troubles or agitates him. One feels that
he is in self-communion with his dreams,
and one involuntarily thinks of a magnifi-
cent lake reflecting the heavens. I have
never witnessed this peaceful reverie
without emotion, without the deep desire
that nothing may trouble or dissipate it.
But little is needed to bring back agita-
tion; the least breath suffices; happy if the
tempest does not break forth. Unfortu-
nately for himself Wagner will never
know the feeling so wisely egotistical—
polite indifference. Before my departure
from Lucerne he wished to organize an
excursion of several days to show us
the country of William Tell. We were
obliged to start at dawn, and the carriage
was winding its way by the lake of Lu-
cerne, or the Four Cantons, when the sun
rose. I remember that a gleam of light
fell upon the master's lips while he was
talking to us. In speaking of Mendelssohn
he said: " He is a great landscape-

painter." I confess to seeing very little of
the country I was visiting. I remember
at the first halting-place a trout upon
which Wagner made a frightful pun,
which I shall not translate. Then came
the steamboat which conveyed us to
Zurich, where the master was welcomed
by the populace as a well-loved king; a
mountain was climbed, a sail followed;
but all is confused. What has ever re-
mained in my memory is the charm of
those days, passed in such glorious in-
timacy, his gentle gayety and simplicity,
the attentive cares, the art of organizing
everything for one's greatest comfort and
pleasure. He was the first to rise and
awake the more slothful ones, and he
hummed the Marseillaise as he tapped
upon our doors.

Once again at Lucerne Wagner con-
fessed that he had been suffering during
the greater part of the journey, but had
been careful to say nothing lest he should

spoil our pleasure. It was with sincere
regret that I finally took leave of my
hosts, being, however, somewhat consoled
by the promise that I should often receive
news from Tribscheu, a promise which
has been faithfully kept. I returned there
the following year, 1870, being at Lu-
cerne when the war was declared. It
was evident with his ardent character
that Wagner could not fail to be deeply
impressed by this event. The idea of a
united Germany impassioned him, and I
confess that I should have loved him less
had he not experienced, like all of us, in
these crises the inspirations of patriotism.
It was deemed expedient, however, not to
touch upon dangerous questions, where we
could not possibly agree, but to remain
prudently in the regions of art, where we
so entirely understood one another. By
this method the events which made us
opponents could not disturb our friendship.
Returned to Paris, the last letter which I

received from him was dated the 5th of
September. 'It informed me of the bap-
tism of his son, to whom I stood god-
mother, but alas, at a distance. "At the
moment of the benediction," he wrote, "a
storm burst upon us with flashes of light-
ning and loud peals of thunder. It appears
that the thunder claps will play their part
in the life of this terrible child. I my-
self like such celestial auguries, while I
hold in aversion those terrestrial blows
which have deprived us of your presence.
I keep to our silence so sensibly agreed
upon. But happily there is a region of
existence where we are and always shall
remain friends. All that separates us,
even in our opinions upon things which
belong to this region, can only con-
tribute to draw us in time nearer and
more intimately together." The horrible
tempest once calmed, we met again with
the same sentiments, each continuing to
reserve his own opinions. In 1872 Lu-

cerne was abandoned for Bayreuth; the great project so long cherished of the theatre built after Wagner's ideas was at last to be realized. The 22d of April Madame Wagner wrote me : "One last word from Tribscheu, my dear friend, which we leave with full hearts and troubled minds. To-morrow Wagner goes to Bayreuth, and I am to follow him with the children and Rus in a week. We cannot, however, leave without sending you our tender remembrances."

The first stone of the theatre was solemnly laid at Bayreuth on the 22d of May of the same year. On this occasion the king sent the following despatch to Wagner : —

"From the depths of my heart, dear friend, I express to you, on this day of such great import to all Germany, my warmest and sincerest congratulations. Success and blessing to the great enter-

prise of the coming year! To-day more
than ever I am with you in spirit."

"LUDWIG."

Beethoven's symphony, with choruses,
directed by Wagner, was the finest
episode of the *fêtes* which followed.
The German public, who knew it well,
was enraptured by the inimitable perfor-
mance. "We cannot express in words
our thanks and admiration for the man-
ner in which Wagner interprets the
works of Beethoven," wrote the Musical
Journal of Berlin. "We have never
heard an orchestra spiritualized to such a
degree. We add our share of enthusiasm
to that of the transported audience." And
Mr. Richard Pohl, a well-known writer,
said: "Richard Wagner, who always
directs without notes, knowing the score
by heart, exercises a marvellous and mag-
netic charm over his orchestra. He forces
it to accomplish his wishes, does with it

what he will, sure of being obeyed. He animates and electrifies each musician, and always remains in sympathetic contact with the whole instrumental body. All divine, so to speak, his thought. He handles the orchestra like a gigantic instrument, with a certainty that never fails him, with a sovereignty before which all joyfully bow. To form an idea of this prodigy it must be witnessed; the revelation is as unique as is Wagner's incomparably artistic nature." "Our *fête* is over," wrote Madame Wagner, several days later, "and in spite of very bad weather it has been superb. The words of Beethoven, 'all men become brothers,' seemed to be realized during these few days at Bayreuth, where our friends, known and unknown, have congregated from every quarter of the globe, having all one thought and one faith."

In 1876 the theatre was finished, and that colossal work, the Ring of the Nibelung, was brought forward and put upon the stage. Sovereigns, artists, an intelligent crowd, rushed toward Bayreuth, which could not contain it, and even the streets were put into requisition for improvised camps. That little city, so completely obscure a few years ago, suddenly rendered famous by the caprice of a man of genius, is hidden behind the chilly mountains of Upper Franconia. · Pine woods, rapid streams, vast plains, bounded by blue-tinted hills against the misty sky, long poplar-studded roads, along which harnessed oxen slowly travel in couples under the brass yoke which forms a sort of crown over their heads, — such is the approach to this once quiet city, which, all at once, in honor of the theatre which rises in proud simplicity on the hill, throws open its gates to welcome emperors, kings, and princes from all countries, and finds itself filled with a joyous crowd, which the innkeepers, waking from their long lethargy, swindle to the best of their ability. While speaking of innkeepers I may recall a characteristic incident which happened at Munich. The hotel-keepers of the city, having previously come to a common understanding, offered to build the projected theatre for Wagner at their own expense, but at Munich, not in Bayreuth. They considered that it would be a great affair for them. Even as a river is diverted from its course, so they proposed to direct toward themselves the tide of visitors; but the master held to Bayreuth and declined their offers.

Wahnfried! Such is the name of Wagner's villa at Bayreuth. Wahnfried, a name full of melancholy doubt, which gives rise to many thoughts, but is difficult to translate; its truest signification being illusions of peace. At the height of his glory, adored almost, he whose life had been so troubled and painful wished to persuade himself that he had at last created, sheltered from all attacks, a retreat where he could thenceforward live in peace; but he himself recognized the futility of this scheme. Can repose exist for such a mind, always pushing irresistibly forward and higher? Folly, illusion, thus to mark a standing-place, to carve one's tombstone, and to dig a grave, while so many desires are still fermenting, and while so many dreams are still outlived, which must be formed, and then again dissipated.

Wahnfried! This word, which at first seemed to me to contain a regret, held, perhaps, on the contrary a hope. The house, constructed upon Wagner's own plan, appears at the end of a long avenue; it is built of grayish red stones, almost square, and without other ornament than the fresco upon the front, which recalls a scene from the Nibelungen. A straight flight of steps leads to the door; that opens upon a small anteroom, which again communicates with a large vestibule, very high, and lighted from the top. It is surrounded, on a level with the first story, by a gallery, decorated with paintings, representing Eastern scenes. The floor is paved with flagstones, divans are placed in the angles, together with marble statues of Wagner's heroes, the work of enthusiastic sculptors, and a large American organ with brass stops. At the right is the dining-room; on the left a little *salon* filled with objects of art. Facing this is the great hall of reunion, vast and sumptuous, at once library and working-room. It is terminated by a glass rotunda opening into the garden, where a fountain is babbling joyously.

The theatre, which stands outside of the city on a hill, is a construction of simple aspect, somewhat resembling the palace of the Trocadéro. When I saw it for the first time rising majestically on the height, illumined by the rays of the setting sun;

when I saw that contemplative crowd
slowly ascending on every side toward this
temple of art, I could not restrain tears of
joy. The dream of this man's entire life
was thus at last realized. The world that
had persecuted him hastened finally to
greet him with a rapture beyond prece-
dent. He, once so persecuted, enjoyed
even in life his apotheosis. This new
phase of his life had changed nothing in
his manner of being; this immense
triumph failed to intoxicate him; he did
not even appear to be greatly impressed.
It seemed to me that the Nibelungen were
far from his mind, which already medi-
tated new creations. He made me visit
the theatre in all its details, from the hid-
den orchestra, sunk beneath the stage, to
the mechanism which held suspended the
Undines of the Rhine. We had to climb
everything that was practicable, descend
to the floor under the stage; and I per-
ceived that the master had lost none of
his agility of Tribscheu.

Those who were present at the admirable representations of 1876, where everything had been prepared and directed by Wagner, will never forget them. A like solemnity has not been reproduced since the great theatrical celebrations of ancient Greece, and will remain a great event in the future history of art. I shall close these few pages, written from memory, by the relation of my last visit to the master, copied from my travelling note book.

BAYREUTH, 29th of September, 1881.

It is with quickly beating hearts that we cross once more the threshold of this dwelling, which, in spite of the cordial reception always awaiting us, we feel to be consecrated ground, the holy of holies, which should not be penetrated without a sort of sacred awe. The whole family is assembled in the drawing-room, which is brightened by a ray of sunlight. Liszt, who has come to pass a few

-weeks with his dear grandchildren, is superb, with his long white hair, his bushy eyebrows, beneath which shine a lion's eyes. My godson is already growing large; he has a broad forehead, and blue eyes of exquisite sweetness. The master comes up from the garden, always the same, even younger. Truly the immortals defy time. He receives us with that tender effusion with which those of his followers, by whom he knows himself perfectly loved, inspire him, for he has nothing of the impassable egotism which so often attacks great men when they arrive at a certain height of glory. He is rather, as we have already said, too impressionable, allows himself to be governed by the momentary violence of his impressions; and the only uneasiness he causes to those who surround him, who live only for him, proceeds from this intensity in his sadness or joy, or from his anger, which a nature less tempered than

his would not be able to resist. He can-
sometimes forget, even completely change,
his opinion, love that which he once de-
tested, and always with the same sincerity.

We pass to the dining-room. The
master is now rapturously gay; he ex-
presses himself with some difficulty in
French, which does not, however, prevent
his playing upon the words as no one else
can. He tells us of his journey to Naples
and Venice, of the pleasure he has de-
rived from Italy, and we quickly divine in
him a longing for the sun and new hori-
zons; he is thinking of Greece, the Bos-
porus, India. Oh Wahnfried, Wahnfried!
One thing evidently wearies him greatly;
it is the instrumentation of Parsifal. He
complains of not being able to form young
artists capable of aiding him in his work;
but this is simply make-believe, he well
knows that it is impossible. "When one
is young," he said, "when the nerves are
not yet fatigued, and one writes scores

with a certain ease, even that of Lohengrin, without knowing all the resources of coloring and combination, the work is not comparable to that which the new works demand, and which must be written at a maturer age. Auber, however, wrote until his eighty-fourth year without fatigue; but he had not changed his manner." Liszt relates a speech of Auber's, to whom a young musician of great promise had been presented. "Are we not enough already?" cried the master. He afterwards spoke of a counterbass with five chords, the object of which is to descend still further in the lower notes than the ordinary counterbass does. Wagner said of a gentleman who came to submit a similar process to him, that he sent him about his business. Mendelssohn, however, has already tried something of the kind and produced a fine effect.

We were reproached for not having come a month sooner, when the house was full of singers, to whom the parts of Parsifal were assigned, and who began their first studies. To console us, Wagner promised to let us hear certain passages. But he pretends to play badly, so that it will not be the same thing. There is a project to go to-morrow to the theatre to see the models of the scenes, provided the machinist who is expected has arrived to show them.

30th September.

We are early to-day at Wahnfried. The gate is never shut except by a bolt, and we can take a solitary walk in the garden without disturbing any one. Long trellises of virgin vines, already blood-stained by the precocious autumn, creep the length of each side of the way leading to the house; it is almost dark under their shelter; in places, however, the green roof becomes lighter, and the dead leaves rustle under our feet. The space intervening between these trellises and the centre walk is reserved for the kitchen garden; but the soil does not appear to be fertile. We come out at the conservatory, where there is already a fire; all the delicate flowers have been brought indoors. A few exotic plants destined to ornament the drawing-room, but which are withering, are there as in an infirmary. In front of the hot-house, on the other side of the house, cries and a flapping of wings indicate the hen-house; it is large and gay, and might be taken for a sample from the garden of acclimation in Paris. Peacocks, silver pheasants, rare hens, and a scattering of pigeons fill it, defying the cook's knife, for the place is as sacred to them as if they were taking their sports within the enclosure of a Brahmin temple.

In front of the drawing-room, and surrounding the fountain, is the pleasure-garden; with fine lawns, beds of Bengal roses, and flowers of all kinds, but many of them are already frostbitten. This free space is enclosed by a bushy wood forming a sort of wall. One must penetrate its shadows to approach the tomb, which has been already so much talked of, and which by a sufficiently exuberant fancy the master caused to be built at the same time with his house. It is completely enveloped by the thick coppice, and is without egress; it is only when autumn strips the trees that a large gray marble slab can be seen through the confusion of branches, over which the briars twine themselves. A graceful pavilion of two stories, a gymnasium for the children, hemicycles of grass, with stone benches, are scattered in this wood, which leads to a little gate, looking out upon the royal residence. The stroke of the clock recalls us to the house. The master has finished his morning task, and shows us his well-filled page lying upon the table. His life is one of the greatest regularity, above all when, as at this time, he is pursuing a hurried and fatiguing work. He rises at six, but after his bath retires again and reads until ten. At eleven he sets himself to work until two o'clock. After dinner he rests for a short time, always in company with a book. From four until six he drives, then goes back to his work until supper, at eight; the evening is passed gayly with his family, and before eleven all the household is in bed.

At table Liszt announces that Darwin declares himself a partisan of vivisection, but that this frightful practice has just been interdicted in England. It is well known that Richard Wagner is one of the warmest defenders of those innocent victims of the physiologist's cruel curiosity. Some time ago he wrote a long article full of sadness and anger, in which he repeats the words of Faust, " The dogs themselves will no longer wish to live in such a world." " Our campaign has already had good results in Germany," he said; "the joiners who manufacture the instruments of torture destined for the unfortunate dogs complain of the dimunition of their sales." He asks us if this humane cause has defenders in France; to which we reply that there are very ardent ones; in the first instance, all honest people: and then we cite among the journalists Victor Meunier, who, in the Rappel, rises vehemently against these cruelties, and very justly compares the actual position of animals to that of the former slaves, over whom their masters were supposed to have every right.

A visit to the theatre is again spoken of; the machinist whom we expected, evidently cannot come; but we shall go to see the models and scenery in M. Ioukouski's studio. "My theatre will, I think," said the master, "become a sort of conservatory where singers will be found, and where the method in which

my works will be executed and put upon
the stage will serve as a model to direct-
ors and managers who will mount them
elsewhere." The Paris Conservatory still
holds to the tradition of the movements
of Gluck's Iphigenia. . . . "You have
there," he added, "an orchestra of the
first order — Beethoven's Symphonies
were played to perfection." Liszt tells of
a very singular appreciation on Boieldieu's
part of the Beethoven Symphonies, at the
time of their first hearing in Paris. "It
certainly produces an effect," he said,
"but it bears a resemblance to people
chewing tobacco and swearing in a guard-
house."

We start upon a visit to M. Paul
Ioukouski's studio. This young painter,
who, meeting Richard Wagner at Naples,
solicited and obtained the honor of being
chosen for the work of the scenery in
Parsifal, and left all to follow the master,
is the son of one of Russia's most illus-

trious poets, who was the preceptor of
Alexander II. The artist is installed in a
house in the immediate neighborhood of
Wahnfried, and lives there like a hermit,
putting his whole heart into his work.
The sketches, which are real pictures, are
displayed upon the various easels. On
the first is the forest, with the rising sun,
for the first tableau, which, to make place
for the second, will slide gently from left
to right, sinking down little by little,
while the characters are supposed to be .
advancing as they ascend a hill. These
characters will disappear behind masses
of rocks, then will be seen again in
grottoes near Cyclopean substructures,
then in galleries. They finally pass through
a door, and the temple of the Grail will
appear.   Here it is seen, upon the neigh-
boring easel, with its porphyry columns, its
capital of precious stones, its vaults, its
double cupolas, its mysterious depths.
The tables destined for the sacred repast,

which bring to mind the sacrament, are arranged on either side of the altar. The smooth marble-paved floor reflects like a lake. Mr. Brandt, machinist of the theatre at Darmstadt, a man of genius, it appears, for whom the word impossible does not exist, says that he can produce this glittering effect, and that the only difficulty lies in the rapid shifting of the scenery.

The fantastic garden, created by the magician, Klingsor, in order to reduce and ruin the Knights of the Grail, was a thing difficult to conceive. Wagner wished for something absolutely improbable; the conception of a dream, a wild efflorescence brought to life by the stroke of a wand, not by plodding earthly labor; he was dissatisfied with every attempt. He has, however, obtained his desire, and it appears that on the stage this scene is one of the most successful of all. What is most singular is that these giant flowers, sheaves, clusters, and thickets, which leave only à corner on the horizon visible, fade away and die in the twinkling of an eye, leaving in sight only an arid moor, shut in by snowy mountains, while a shower of withered leaves and dried petals falls upon the ground. The flowering meadow near the spring wood, which shelters the hermit's hut, with its clear spring murmuring beneath the thick moss, is truly enchanting. From this we return by a shifting of scenes analogous to that in the first act, to the temple of the Grail, where the piece ends. The costumes are not more easy of invention, for the master will not be satisfied with anything like the costumers' indignation. Even should they all become wretched they must yield. The enchantresses evoked by the magician,— women who are flowers, as the syrens are fishes, — are those who give the most trouble. Wagner will not have attractive young girls, but real animated flowers. There is also the

tunic of the terrible and marvellous
Kundry.

1st October.

The master has kept his promise this
evening, and has let us hear fragments
from Parsifal. "Liszt's presence makes
me lose my powers in a measure," he
said, laughing, "he intimidates me, for I
know that my false notes irritate him."
Unfortunately, Liszt, who only yester-
day improvised upon the piano in a
delightful manner, blending with his own
inventions motions from Tristan and
Isolde, has slightly wounded his finger,
and cannot play. It must certainly be
acknowledged that Wagner is an imper-
fect pianist, and he is the first to laugh at
his own imperfection. We notice, how-
ever, in a wonderful manner, certain pas-
sages which the author knows how to
render with the true expression, better
than any other. A few months ago, Liszt
wrote to us: " Wagner has worked a new

miracle, Parsifal. Those who already have the good fortune to understand this new work share this opinion; the singers are enraptured. Judging from the general impression, this ought to be a new transformation in the master's method, — one of those giant steps to which he is accustomed. In this instance the height and refinement of art combine to produce an effect of apparent simplicity and perfect serenity." This evening we take leave of our illustrious hosts, promising to meet them again next year at the first representation of Parsifal.

POETIC WORK.

WAGNER'S POETIC WORK.

THE spectacle, which represents a series of lofty and still loftier peaks of a chain of mountains, at the moment when the morning mists envelop them, furnishes a just comparison to that given us by these works, which rise successively, one above the other, from the lovely green hill to the dazzling and, for many, inaccessible summits. From Rienzi to the Gloom of the Gods there is the same difference of attitude as between the Capitoline Hill and the Himalaya. And what gigantic strides from one work to the other. A powerful, enthusiastic genius already reveals itself in Rienzi; but it has done little more than assimilate, with the greatest facility, the

65

beauties that had most charmed one in the works of its predecessors. Wagner likes show, pompous processions, the tumult of battle; the brilliant orchestra resounds, is carried away, enthusiastic; the power which moves it, not yet under control, expends itself in vociferations, heroic cries of extreme vehemence; but as yet nothing presages the innovator, if it be not the almost prophetic sense of the subject, so ardently revolutionary.

Between Rienzi and The Flying Dutchman lies an abyss. The young master, disdaining the success of his first work, judges it with severity and casts it aside; he considers it an essay. From the first he has equalled his models, but he feels that he is still far from his ideal; a new world palpitates in his mind; he must break the old moulds and fetters of routine that he may soar untrammelled toward unexplored regions. The artist, now sure of himself, definitely abandons historical subjects, whose too hard reality is not in keeping with the idealism of music. The natural poetry of legend and myth suits him far better. Henceforward the path is found, he will no longer turn aside from it, but continually enlarge upon its thought. From the popular song, hummed by the Norwegian spinners while turning their wheels, he will rise to the savage grandeurs of the northern theogonies. It was upon a sea-voyage, during a storm, which cast him upon the coast of Norway, that Richard Wagner induced the sailors themselves to repeat to him the frightful story of the Flying Dutchman — Ahasverus of the Sea, who, blaspheming, defied the storm with Satan's aid, and was condemned to wander eternally, he and his fantastic ship. But the mystical young girl, grown pale from the snow's reflections, who languishes with love for the damned one, carried incessantly through shipwrecks and lightning, will save him by her faithful devotion, even unto death, if he but reaches her.

This work seems to have come at a single stroke, under the inspiration of a violent emotion. The ocean, with its rage, its awe, its mystery and sweetness — all is in this music, which is like the sea's own soul. If a few traces of the old formulæ remain, it is only in the subordinate parts of the work. The orchestra is no longer a great guitar, accompanying a song; it already assumes a capital importance; the designs, dividing and blending, have a precise meaning; the whole, less noisy, acquires a power until then unknown. The orchestral tissue becomes the woof upon which the characters are embroidered; it becomes the ocean which bears the ship, the atmosphere which envelops the action, where the thoughts, the sentiments of the heroes, reverberating, amplifying, become visible, so to speak, and make the mind experience all that is inexpressible in the sensations of the soul.

The legend of Tanhäuser still exists in Germany, above all in leafy Thuringia, where the famous castle of Wartburg stands, which, under the hospitable land-graves of the thirteenth century, was the theatre of pacific contests, fought by the illustrious troubadours. In front of the castle rises a bare, dreary mountain, burned as it were, which makes a strange blot in the midst of the fresh vegetation of the neighboring valleys. This is the ter-rible Venusberg, inhabited, according to popular tradition, by a dangerous goddess. This divinity was formerly Hulda the beneficent, who came each year to awaken the spring, and wandered over the country scattering flowers under her feet. But being cursed by Christianity, she was obliged to take refuge in the unknown caverns of the mountain; she was soon confounded with Venus, the sovereign of the senses. The graces, syrens, bacchantes, and fauns constituted her court, and enchanting voices seduced those whose impure desires guided them toward the mountain; unknown roads enticed them, and they were borne away to the mysterious palace which it encloses, in the abode of eternal perdition, from which none return. The Knight Tanhäuser, curious and intrepid, found the path of the grottoes in the Venusberg, and was the spouse of the goddess during seven years, after which, his desires satiated and himself devoured with remorse, aspiring to human suffering, he succeeded in tearing himself from the arms of his love by invoking the Virgin Mary. He went and confessed to the pope, imploring his pardon, but the pontiff replied, " that having tasted the pleasures of hell he was forever damned." Then raising his crosier, he added, "Even as this wood cannot become green again, so is there no pardon for thee." The legend adds, that at the expiration of three days the crosier began to blossom, signifying that celestial grace is greater than that of a pontiff. It is from this recital, enlarged by a powerful spirit, that Wagner has taken his drama, interweaving with his own tissue the tradition about the famous contests of the poet-singers, and also the chaste and melancholy face of Elisabeth, whom he voluntarily confounds with the sainted princess whose virtuous life shed a lustre over the the castle. But what Richard Wagner has above all wished to bring out in this marvellous work is the eternal struggle between the flesh and the spirit, the brute and the angel, which, being in man, dispute his soul. And this he has rendered with incomparable clearness and grandeur. The discussions formerly raised by the representation of Tanhäuser have made this debated work better known than many others illustrious from success.

It is useless, therefore, to speak of it further.

Lohengrin, which has never been represented in Paris, and which can scarcely be appreciated from partial executions of the most inferior order, is, strange to say, almost popular. Whoever has heard the orchestral prelude typifying the vision of King Titurel, when the angels bring to him the Holy Grail, can never forget this admirable passage, and the extraordinary impression which it produces. At first an almost imperceptible vibration takes possession of the highest notes of the flutes and violins. The air becomes agitated, the light approaches and grows larger, soon with an irradiation of trumpets the luminous vision shines resplendent in all its glory. The incomparable cup, cut from a stone, it is said, which fell from Lucifer's crown when he was precipitated from heaven, and which is now filled with the blood of the Saviour, is confided to the pure hands of a holy knight. Then the angels again take their flight, the glimmering becomes obliterated, and the atmospheric vibrations, which can no longer be heard, little by little diminish and die away. The curtain rises upon a site near the environs of Anvers, on the borders of Scheldt. We find ourselves in the tenth century. Henry the Fowler, King of Germany, has come to Brabant to convoke the noble lords according to the feudal custom. Frederick of Telramund, the most valiant of all the lords of Brabant, has just accused, before all the people, Elsa, Duchess of Brabant, of the murder of her young nrother, who has disappeared, leaving no trace. The young girl possesses no method of proving her innocence; her cause then is to be submitted to the judgment of God. But when the herald has resounded the trumpet toward the four quarters of the world, no knight has entered the lists in her defence. Elsa, however, has con-

fidence in a singular vision: a charming
warrior has appeared to her in a dream;
he will fight for her. However, the
herald's second summons remains without
response. It is then that, with an impulse
of sublime faith, she throws herself upon
her knees, and beseeches Heaven to send
her the defender who has visited her in a
vision.

Soon, in fact, the people, grouped upon
the banks of the river, see in the distance,
with increasing agitation, a strange bark
drawn by a dazzling swan; it approaches,
it draws nearer; a knight of wondrous
beauty stands erect in the bark; his light
helmet, his silver breastplate are resplen-
dent, he rests one hand upon his shield.
"A miracle! a miracle!" cries the
crowd. "Can it be an angel sent by
God?" The mysterious knight steps
upon the shore. With a calm and modest
voice he bids farewell to the beautiful
swan which has conducted him and now

returns to the unknown regions from which it came. Then the knight advances in the midst of the surprised and rejoicing multitude. "I am come," he says, "to defend the innocent girl unjustly accused. Who will do combat with me?" Telramund, notwithstanding the sacred character of his adversary, and preferring death to dishonor, raises the gauntlet and upholds the accusation. The knight draws near the enraptured Elsa, and in a sweet, grave voice, says to her: "If I bear off the victory, wilt thou that I should become thy husband? Then must thou promise never to seek to discover from what countries I come, nor what is my name or nature." "My shield, my angel, my savior!" cried Elsa, "thou who defendest me in my distress, how could I do other than faithfully keep to the law thou imposest upon me?" "Elsa, I love thee," murmurs the unknown knight with deepest tenderness. The king blesses

the arms, and the combat begins. The
knight gains an easy victory over his
adversary, whose life he spares. Elsa's
innocence is proclaimed by the entire
people in a triumphal hymn of joy.

But Ortrud, Telramund's wife, daugh-
ter of the King of Friesia, who aspires to
the throne of Brabant, succeeds in excit-
ing feminine curiosity in Elsa, and in pour-
ing the poison of doubt into her heart in
order to blight her joy. She torments her
until at last Elsa, distracted, violates her
oath, exacting from her spouse the avowal
of his origin. Doubt has killed faith, which
carries with it all happiness; the night of
love ends in despair. It is upon a meadow
near the border of the Scheldt, amid flying,
banners and flourishing trumpets, in the
presence of Brabant counts, followed by
their vassals called by King Henry for an
expedition against the Hungarians, that
the mysterious knight will unveil his ori-
gin. "In a distant country," he says,

"upon a high mountain, called Mont Sal-
vat, stands a magnificent temple, in which
knights of absolute purity guard a mirac-
ulous cup; it is the Holy Grail, the cup in
which Christ consecrated the bread and
wine at the time of the Lord's Supper, and
in which, later, Joseph of Arimathea re-
ceived his blood. This cup had been car-
ried to heaven by the angels, but they
brought it back again to the holy king,
Titurel, who founded the temple of the
Grail, and the order of its knights. Those
who serve the Grail are endowed with
wonderful virtue, but an inflexible law
forces them to remain unknown among
men. If their name be discovered, they
must immediately depart, and once more
regain the sacred mountain. For this rea-
son I must leave you, informing you that
Parsifal, my father, is King of the Grail,
and I, his knight, am named Lohengrin."
The swan reappears upon the shore to
bear the warrior away to his miraculous

country; Elsa has destroyed her happiness; she sees her guardian angel depart forever.

Lohengrin is, perhaps, the most perfect of the three lyric dramas which form the second period in the master's work. From Lohengrin to Tristan and Isolde as great a distance is marked as between Rienzi and the Flying Dutchman. It is a new revelation, a new art, — something perfect and definite, a prodigious flight toward the future. There is no longer, so to speak, any question of music in the sense formerly attached to this word; it is poetry in superb and precise form, with a sonorous resonant soul, — Apollo and Orpheus melted in a single lyre. The works following may, perhaps, be grander, but Tristan and Isolde is and will remain the masterpiece of masterpieces, by reason of the poetical subject which, in art as in the human soul, takes by right the first place. In Tristan and Isolde love itself,

in its most complete and perfect form,
finds utterance. The most pointed phases
of the passion are pushed to their extreme.
In the first act it is unavailing love, hero-
ically conquered, which consumes the
heart while not a cry escapes the lips, —
Tristan, conducting toward another the
royal betrothed, whose hand he himself,
in his blind love, has solicited for the King
of Cornwall. Tristan's love believes it-
self despised. Isolde, consumed with an-
ger and tenderness, powerless to master
the tumult in her soul, wishes shipwreck
to the vessel which bears her away,
with the hero who disdains her, toward
the shore which she hopes never to reach.
" Death rather, death for us both! " she
cries. And when the tempest betrays her,
when already the hated land is signaled,
she offers poison.

Tristan cannot refuse to empty a cup in
Isolde's honor, to drink to their recon-
ciliation, for a debt of blood lies between

them, long since effaced by their un-
avowed love, but which she begins to re-
member. Tristan well knows that eternal
forgetfulness is poured out for him by the
hand which he secretly adores; he ac-
cepts with gratitude this mitigation of
evils which have no remedy. On the
threshold of death, however, both drop
their mask, the fire then breaks out tri-
umphant, love casts them into one another's
arms in the intoxication of a supreme joy
which should repay them for their past
sufferings. Heart against heart, eyes
looking into eyes, thus will their hearts
cease to beat, and their mutual gaze be
extinguished. But alas! they are betrayed;
the two devoted followers have substituted
for the mortal draught a love-drink, and
instead of the kindly shade which reunited
them, behold the detested shore, and the
deceitful day which separates them.

Such a love once free can no longer
be stifled or conquered. It is a formid-

able conflagration, a flame which death
itself cannot extinguish. It has devoured
everything, — loyalty, honor, virtue. The
earth itself becomes effaced in the ravish-
ing rapture of mutual possession. Infinite
and sublime ecstasy follows, which no
heart can have either experienced or fore-
seen. Their happiness even crushes and
stifles them; the heart cannot contain such
love, the human voice has no words to
express it; the most burning embraces
leave them disunited. Tristan and Isolde
are two, and they would become one soul,
a single thought, a scintillation of love in
an unlimited night. Desperate and un-
satisfied, they aspire to the infinity of
death. They dream of a flight beyond all
worlds in that mysterious shade which
protects them upon earth, but over which
the day and the empty phantoms of life
triumph, ceaselessly inflicting the tortures
of impending separation. The eternal
and great night of love without the terrors

of the morning! A long enchanting dream
in unlimited space; no names to separate;
a single flame; a single thought; a sweet
swoon in each other's arms; the ardent
rapture 'of death without end, without
awakening! Such is their thought. But
suddenly, behold the cruel day, and with
it shame. This sublime love is dragged
before the world, which calls it an indis-
cretion, and censures. Then follows the
combat, in which Tristan, overcome with
a divine ecstasy, is no longer the victorious
hero, but falls mortally wounded.

When we see him again, in the agonies
of death, it is in the ancient dungeon of
his ancestors in Brittany. The faithful
shield-bearer has taken him across the
seas in a bark. Now he is sheltered from
all surprise. But Isolde? When his eyes,
which seem to be forever closed, will
awake to life, if they are not gladdened by
his soul's sweet sovereign, they will close
again forever. Isolde knows her loved

one's retreat; she is coming to him, but the
minutes are centuries, and the sea is de-
serted and void, even to the silent horizon.
See, the hero now comes to himself with
the dear name upon his lips. Tristan can-
not die while Isolde is still in the empire of
the sun. The gates of death, which had
already closed upon him with a clang,
reopen wide before this invincible desire
to see once more her with whom alone he
can lose himself in eternal night. Void and
deserted is the sea! Thus it is that the
fury of despair tears Tristan's soul. Love
and fever mingling their delirium, he
writhes upon his bed of pain with cries of
superhuman suffering. Nothing can ren-
der the impression of this frightful agony,
in which the flame of love cannot be ex-
tinguished by death, of this distracted and
expectant soul, retarding the supreme de-
parture. At intervals the hero falls to the
ground, seemingly dead; but when the
weeping shield-bearer stoops to hear a last

sigh, a last palpitation, Tristan in a low voice
murmurs the name of Isolde! Yet once
again hope springs to life in the breast of
this martyr to love; he perceives the ship,
although common eyes cannot distinguish
it, and on the ship Isolde, who makes a sign
to him. "Dost thou not see it yet? Tender
and majestic she crosses the breadth of
the sea like a sovereign; she comes carried
toward land as by waves of intoxicating
flowers; her smile will pour out supreme
consolation. Oh, Isolde! Isolde! how
beautiful, how welcome art thou!" The
ship is, in truth, signalled. The soul's
eyes are not deceived. All sails spread,
it flies over the waters. She approaches
— she, the enchanting one, she comes.
What delirious impatience, what joyous
transports!

"Intoxication of the soul, rapture without
measure, impetuous and overheated blood,
how shall I support you chained to this
couch? Up then, up, on the march toward

the beating heart!" Already Isolde's voice is heard, and the hero throws himself, staggering, from his bed. She comes, she calls him, holds her arms toward him; but he can only die at her feet, uttering for the last time the infinitely-beloved name. "Ah, live with me yet one hour, only an hour," cries the distracted Isolde in her despair. "I have only lived through so many days of anguish and desire to watch one hour with thee. Do not die of thy wound, let me heal thee, that safe and strong we may share the sainted delights of night." The flame is extinguished, the soul has fled. Isolde, always faithful, will follow Tristan in death. Already the loved one. draws her toward the mysterious land; mighty waves seem to overpower her. Her ears resound with murmurs of the infinite. Night, consoling night, gently envelops her, overwhelms her. She is drowned, lost, to unite herself forever to the twin flame, and loses her-

self in the divine breath of the universal
soul. It is almost impossible to imagine
the intensity of expression which this
poem, so passionate, so intense in itself,
acquires united to the magic of music.
It is like the vital energy of the soul, a
supernatural rapture. The intoxication
and the acute torments experienced in
hearing this work are ineffaceable. All
who have entered into its transcendent
beauties, and undergone its terrible charm
in all its power, recognize that no other
artistic impression is comparable to that
which makes itself felt in this extraor-
dinary work. Many volumes in all lan-
guages have been written upon Tristan
and Isolde; many will still be written, for
it is the magnificent prerogative of a great
masterpiece to be the perpetual inspiration
of noble minds.

THE MASTERSINGERS OF NUREMBURG.

The scene of this piece is laid in the sixteenth century, at that singular epoch when art and poetry, disdained by the nobility, had taken refuge among the citizens and trades-people. Since the disappearance of the Minnesingers, those minstrels of love so closely resembling the French troubadours, the Mastersingers alone taught poetry and music. These masters were also chiefs of corporations, and their scholars, at the same time their apprentices, learned to stitch a sole and hold a note, to scan a verse and cut a pair of breeches. It is easy to imagine in what degree art must have languished in such a state, how the many rules and laws of these narrow-minded men must have trammelled the flight of inspiration, which must of necessity fold its wings and walk in trodden paths. It was like a bird brought up by

a mole. If by chance a new-comer, pos-
sessing no science save his own genius,
ventured into the circle of poet-mechanics,
it is easy to imagine what a concert of im-
precations assailed the freedom with which
he broke the laws, minutely woven by
routine, as if they had been spiders' webs.
It is an event of this nature which Richard
Wagner has chosen to form the plot of
his comedy.

Walter von Stolzing, a knight of Fran-
conia, is in love with the daughter of
Pogner, a rich goldsmith of Nuremberg;
but only he who shall be proclaimed mas-
tersinger at the next competition shall
obtain the hand of Eva. Walter, who
does not know the first word of art, wishes
to compete. He endeavors to gain a little
information from the untutored David,
pupil and apprentice of Hans Sachs. The
scene passes in the aisles of the church
named after St. Catherine in Nuremberg,
which the apprentices are about arranging

for the masters' meeting. "So you wish to become master?" says David to Walter. "It is so difficult then?" "The art of a master cannot be acquired in a day. Here I have been a whole year with the greatest man in Nuremberg, Hans Sachs, who teaches me poetry and shoemaking at the same time; when I have tanned the leather well, he makes me repeat the vowels and consonants; when I have waxed the thread well he makes me understand rhyme. Well, where do you imagine I am now?" "Perhaps you have made a good pair of buskins?" "Oh, no, I am not so far advanced yet," cries the apprentice. "Let us see; do teach me," says Walter. "Very well; know then that the masters' tones and modes are numerous, and that each has its name; there is the long tone, and the too long tone, the mode of writing-paper, the sweet tone, and the rose tone, the tone of short love, and the forgotten tone, the mode of English zinc, of the cinnamon stalk, of frogs, of calves, the mode of the deceased glutton, and of the faithful pelican, and so through a long, long chapter. "Good heavens, what is all that," cried the terrified Walter. "But it is not enough to know the names," continued David, "one must understand how to sing each mode without changing what they call the figuration and the tabulature. For myself, I am not yet so far advanced, and my master often sings the mode of the martinet to me, and unless my good friend Magdalene comes to my assistance I myself sing the mode of dry bread and water. Know then that a mastersinger is he who composes a new mode in poetry and music."

Poor Walter is bewildered. His love, however, prevents him from renouncing his project, and when Pogner advances, accompanied by Beckmesser, a grotesque scrivener, who also aspires to Eva's hand, Walter draws near his beloved one's

father, and informs him of his desire to
compete. Soon the Mastersingers as-
semble to deliberate in regard to the pub-
lic competition of the morrow. Among
the odd physiognomies of the poet-
mechanics the handsome face of Hans
Sachs, the illustrious poet-shoemaker,
stands out in fair relief. Pogner presents
the young gentleman to his brother artists,
announcing that he wishes to take part in
the competition. A cry is immediately
heard: "In what school have you studied?
who are you masters?" "When, in the
depths of winter," said Walter, "the
snow covered the court and castle, seated
in a corner of the tranquil fireplace, I
read an old book which spoke to me of
the charms of spring; then soon the spring-
time came, and what this book had taught
me during the cold nights I heard re-
sound in the forests and fields: it is
then that I learned to sing." Imagine
what shouts and shoulder-shrugs greeted

this audacity. He is invited, however, to
give a specimen of his talent. He must
improvise something; but should he offend
the rules more than seven times, his work
will be declared unacceptable. The
marker, or marksman, armed with slate
and pencil, already steps into the box,
where he is to shut himself up to listen
to the song, and mark down the faults.
This marker is Beckmesser, the com-
petitor and rival of Walter. "Begin,"
he sings out from the back of his place.
Walter seizes this word, which is cast at
him like a defiance.

"Begin!" he exclaims, "it is the cry
uttered to Nature by Spring, and her
powerful voice resounds in the forests, in
the thickets; the distant echoes reverberate
them. Then everything awakes and be-
comes animated. Songs, perfumes, colors
are born of this cry." All the joy with
which the birth of spring can fill a young
man's heart, sings in Walter's voice. But

the rules, what has he done with them?
and the tabulature, — the rules laid down
in the tables? At each instant the pencil
is heard grating upon the slate, and
soon even the marker springs furiously
from his box, declaring that there is no
more room on his tablet. Then every
tongue is set loose, and all vent their
anger upon the young knight; he has
heaped error upon error, folly upon folly;
he does not know the first word of art.
"He even rose hurriedly from his seat,"
cries one master, at the end of his argu-
ments. In the midst of this tumult, which
becomes formidable, Walter resumes his
free and joyous song, as if to protest, in
the name of reviving nature, against this
glacial breath of blighting winter. The
frolicsome apprentices, delighted with
this confusion, surround the furious as-
sembly in a wild round dance, and ironi-
cally wish that Walter may get the
betrothal bouquet.

The second act shows us one of the picturesque streets of ancient Nuremberg. Hans Sachs' shop opens upon one side, while on the other stands Pogner's house. Sachs returns from the tumultuous sitting in a thoughtful mood; he alone has been deeply moved by the young knight's improvisation, and feels his old beliefs wavering. "Ah," he cries, while the orchestra rehearses again and again fragments of Walter's song, "I cannot retain this melody, nor yet can I forget it; it was new, and yet it sounded like an old song." He enters his house and sets himself at work before the open window. Eva, who loves the young knight, comes and surprises Hans Sachs, and tries to obtain information from him in regard to the meeting, and the manner in which Walter was received. "Oh, as far as that goes, all is lost!" cries Sachs. "My child, he who is born master will not make his fortune among masters; let him

go elsewhere in search of happiness."
"Yes, he will find it elsewhere," cries the
young girl, angrily; " near hearts which
still burn with a generous flame in spite
of envious and crafty masters." Walter
comes back, still quivering with rage; he
wishes to carry off his beloved and
marry her in his castle. It is nightfall, the
hour is propitious, the street deserted.
Eva consents to follow her lover; but
Hans Sachs, who watches over the two,
sets his shutters ajar, and lets the light of
his lamp fall upon them; a luminous trail
bars the way; the two lovers are made
prisoners by this ray.

Moreover, here is Beckmesser, who ap-
pears armed with a guitar; he imagines
that a serenade will dispose Eva's heart
favorably, and he begins a prelude. Sachs,
for his part, has carried his bench outside,
and resumes his work; by this arrange-
ment he can better overlook the lovers.
He attends to his work with all his might,

and strikes up a noisy song, to the infinite displeasure of the serenader. Several windows are already half opened, and inquisitive heads are thrust out to inform themselves of what is going on. Beckmesser will not yield; he sings louder and louder to drown Sachs's voice, who will not, on his part, be silenced. The confusion becomes extraordinary, the awakened inhabitants come in haste from every side, and David, who thinks that the serenade is intended for his friend Magdalene, Eva's servant, falls upon the singer with clenched fists. Pitchers of water are thrown from the windows upon the heads of the noisemakers; the delighted apprentices come to increase the confusion; every one speaks at once; they become exasperated, and quarrel; blows are given at random, and the squabble becomes general.

All at once a trumpet sounds in the distance, and the crowd disperses as if by magic; each one takes refuge in his own house, the windows are again closed, and the night-watch, rubbing his eyes, persuaded that he has been dreaming, advances in the deserted street. "The eleventh hour has struck," he sings, "guard yourselves against spirits and hobgoblins." The moon, meanwhile, shows its broad face behind a pointed gable. The curtain rises again upon the interior of Hans Sachs's house. Walter, who has passed the night under the shoemakers roof, enters the studio, worn out and discouraged, for the day which is dawning is that of the festival and competition. All hope of gaining Eva is thus lost. "Come, come," says Sachs, "do not give up yet; make me a poem upon the dream, for example, which has traversed your brain during the night." The young man obeys, and Sachs writes the verses. upon a sheet of paper, which he designedly leaves upon the table while both go to prepare themselves for the

festival. They are hardly gone when
Beckmesser arrives, still covered with
bruises from the night's battle, of which
the orchestra wickedly reminds him. His
eyes light upon the sheet of paper; he
reads the verses and imagines that Sachs
also wishes to compete and aspire to
Eva's hand. When the shoemaker re-
turns, Beckmesser reproaches him bitterly
on this score and overwhelms him with
sarcasms.

"What is the matter with you?" says
Sachs, laughing. "I have never dreamed
of competing, and as these verses please
you, I give them to you; do with them
what you will." Beckmesser, thinking
the verses those of Sachs, the most skil-
ful master of Nuremberg, joyously carries
off the fortunate manuscript, sure of vic-
tory. Eva, beautifully adorned for the
festival, but with a sad, pale face, enters
Sachs' studio as she passes. She has
made a pretext of her shoe, which hurts

her, she pretends; but Sachs well knows
where the shoe pinches, in spite of the
reproaches she addresses to him for
not divining it. While kneeling before
her the shoemaker holds her prisoner,
one foot shoeless, and pretends to rectify
the shoe in which she finds so many faults.
Walter comes out of the bedroom, and
stands dazzled at the head of the staircase
before the young girl, more beautiful than
ever in her betrothal dress. Then en-
thusiastically he improvises the last strophe
of his song. Eva, palpitating with sur-
prise and emotion, holds her breath as she
listens. " Well, does the shoe fit at last? "
says Sachs, in a troubled voice. Eva
understands the good shoemaker is her
friend and ally, and throws herself weep-
ing into his arms.

After a short interlude, the curtain rises
again upon the site where the festival is
to be held. It is on the border of the
river in which Nuremberg reflects its

pointed roofs, towers, and ramparts; in a
vast meadow which extends along the
banks.   Peasants and citizens arrive from
every quarter; joyous companies dis-
embark from flag-bedecked boats ; the
corporations advance with the flourish of
the city trumpets; the apprentices, gayly
decorated, add their enthusiasm to the
merry tumult; they clasp nimble young
girls about the waist and dance a rustic
waltz upon the grass.   But a rumor
in the crowd announces the arrival
of the Mastersingers.   Silence is estab-
lished, and the masters make their appear-
ance in great style.   The charming Eva
is near her father, holding in her hand the
crown destined for the conqueror.   Hans
Sachs appears in his turn.   Upon seeing
him, a prolonged tremor runs through the
assembly; the crowd cannot contain its
joy; the people's favorite is received with
loud acclamations, and by a sudden in-
spiration every voice chants the song

with which Hans Sachs greeted Luther, and the dawn of the Reformation: —

> Rouse thyself ; the day is breaking ;
> A voice rises from the coppice :
> I hear the song of the nightingale,
> It resounds from summit to summit,
> In the valley and in the field.
> The night is sinking in the west,
> Red dawn is gleaming in the east,
> And the sad cloud takes flight.

It is difficult to give an idea of the power of this piece, which seems to embody all human aspirations toward liberty.

The competition begins. Beckmesser, who has not understood one word of Walter's poetry, scans it after his manner, and sings upon the grotesque motives of his serenade. He becomes so perplexed that the crowd, at first surprised, breaks out in a loud peal of laughter. "After all," said the singer, spitefully, "the verses are not mine, but Sachs's."

"Well, then, let Walter sing them," says Hans Sachs. The knight's youth and grace impress the people favorably, and when his pure voice resounds, and the poetry is heard in its own form, acclamations break forth on every side. The masters themselves, disturbed, cannot conceal their emotion. The enthusiasm is general.

The happy conqueror, transported with joy, kneels before his loved one, who, trembling, lays upon his head the crown of laurels.

THE RING OF THE NIBELUNG.

INTRODUCTORY: RHINEGOLD.

WHEN the curtain rises there are seen through a bluish penumbra the vague depths of a stream, bristling here and there with black rocks; a peaceful undulation agitates the water, which seems to be

flowing slowly. Suddenly a voice re-
sounds, and an Undine, gliding from 'the
heights, swims in circles about a reef, on
the summit of which a gold nugget glitters;
then two other daughters of the Rhine
glide into the water, and all three chase
one another as they play about the all-
powerful gold, as yet virgin and untouched.
But see! from the river's obscure depths
clambers an odd dwarf, who follows the
Undines' charming game with eager eyes.
He frightens them at first. But they soon
laugh at their fears, perceiving that the
dwarf is in love with them. They make
sport of him by pursuing him, tempting
him, then escaping from him, defying him
with their mocking laughter. The sun
now passes above the stream, a ray falls
upon the gold nugget, which suddenly
shines resplendent, and illumines the water
to its depths. " What is that? " cries the
astonished Nibelung. " What," they re-
ply, " thou knowest naught of the marvel-

lous gold? He who will be able to forge
a ring of this gold shall gain the heritage
of the world; but in order to acquire this
power, he must first renounce love. For
this reason we have no fear that our play-
thing will be taken from us, for every one
who lives loves. None will renounce the
delights of love, and less than any other,
Alberich the Nibelung, who is almost
dying of amorous desires."

But the dwarf has listened with pro-
found attention to the Undines' prattle,
which has so imprudently disclosed the
secret of the gold. He climbs from sum-
mit to summit, slips, falls back again, be-
comes infuriated, but soon cries in a ter-
rible voice, "Scoff now, perfidious spirits,
you will sport henceforward in obscurity,
for I shall tear the miraculous gold from the
rock. I will forge the avenging ring, and
let these waters hear me: I curse love."
And the dwarf plunges and disappears
with his luminous prey, pursued by the

disconsolate Undines. The entire stream sinks with them and slowly lays bare the summit of a mountain where the gods are sleeping. On the top of the neighboring mountain, which little by little emerges from the morning vapors, appears, gilded by the morning sun, a strange and formidable castle. It is the Walhalla, the magnificent stronghold which the giants have just finished for the gods. Wotan and Fricka, upon awakening, contemplate it with joy and surprise; but the goddess is anxious; the rude laborers will claim their reward. Wotan has imprudently promised them Frya, the sweet divinity of love. The task now being finished, it must be paid for. It is Loge, the genius of fire, who has taken it upon himself to find Frya's ransom; he appears at last, the mocking god; but he has explored earth and heaven in vain. In no place has he discovered that which can surpass the charms of love. One being only has given preference to the dominion of gold, stolen by him from the daughters of the Rhine.

The giants have lent their ear to this recital, and the desire to possess this gold is aroused in them. Let them be given this all-powerful metal, and they will relinquish the fair Frya; meanwhile they carry away the charming goddess, who weeps and supplicates. Then the heavens become darkened; a mortal affliction has taken possession of the gods. Old age has suddenly come upon them; Fricka totters, Wotan droops his head, the god of joy sees the roses of his crown fading, Thor no longer has his flashes of anger; the hammer which makes the lightning burst forth drops from his hand; youth, beauty, love are gone with Frya. Wotan suddenly resolves to go and conquer this longed-for gold. Accompanied by Loge, he descends to the gloomy kingdom, where the gnomes forge their metals ceaselessly. He soon gains the mastery

over the Nibelung, possessor of the gold,
which has already brought into subjection
all the blacksmiths, and he carries him off
with his treasures to the mountain of the
gods. But the despoiled Nibelung still
remains in possession of the all-powerful
ring. He presses it between his fingers
in supreme despair. It is in vain. Wo-
tan wrests it from him, after which he
leaves him free to return to the bowels of
the earth. The vanquished Nibelung then
rises, full of fury and despair. "May this
ring be forever cursed!" he cries; "mis-
fortune to the possessor of the gold; may
he who has it not covet it with rage; may
he who possesses it retain it in the an-
guish of fear; cursed! cursed!" and he
replunges into the night of the Nibelung's
home.

Frya has returned, and with her have
joy and youth. The giants lay the Nibe-
lung's gold before her. They desire a
heap large enough to cover the goddess.

She disappears, indeed, but her glance, like a star's ray, darts through an interstice. Alas! the treasure is exhausted; the ring only remains, which will just fill the fissure, but Wotan will not give it up. The gods entreat in vain, when a solemn voice is heard, and in a pale light slowly appears the ancient Erda, the pallid divinity, older than the world, from whom nothing is hidden. "Yield, Wotan," she says, "fly the cursed ring; I know what has been; I know what should be. Hearken! All that exists will have its end. A time will come when a sinister gloom will descend upon the gods. Separate thyself from the cursed ring, and reflect with terror." Erda disappears. Wotan, full of anxiety, casts the ring from him. Pride and strength, however, are now restored to the gods. Thor brandishes his hammer, and in a formidable and joyous voice invokes the wind and the clouds. The heavens become overcast, the lightning flashes, the thunder peals with a crash, and, while the rain descends in heavy drops, the Walhalla is disclosed on the mountain summit, and the rainbow stretches its semi-circle above the valley. The gods take the direction of this luminous bridge to enter into possession of the castle, which glitters in the setting sun. Then plaintive voices rise from the valley; it is the daughters of the Rhine lamenting their brilliant plaything; but the piercing music from the divine castle overpowers the Undines' voices, and the gods triumphant enter the Walhalla.

FIRST DAY: THE WALKYRIA.

Here begins the human drama. Wotan is troubled since Erda's sinister prediction, feeling that the shameful traffic which Walhalla has cost him has lessened his divinity and disturbed the world's equilibrium. Wotan has engendered a race of men of whom a hero shall be born, who by his own force will wrest the gold from the giants and restore it to its primeval place, thus expiating the fault of the gods. Sigmund is the hero chosen by Wotan for this redemption. When the curtain rises upon the second act it discloses the interior of a habitation of the early ages. A venerable ash raises its enormous trunk in the centre of the hall, and its verdant branches, extending in every direction, support the canvas roof. A large stone serves as fireplace; on the bare ground are spread skins of wild beasts; the gate is a high door made of the trunks of trees. The tempest rages without. Sigmund, who seems to be pursued by the angry heavens, enters staggering, and falls exhausted near the fireplace.

A young woman, attracted by the noise, appears, and bends over the stranger with compassionate surprise. Then, to revive him, she offers him a horn of mead. Sig-

mund raises his eyes toward her; their
glances meet and remain fixed upon one
another with an emotion rich with trouble.
But the young man suddenly raises him-
self. " Farewell! farewell! " he cries, " I
bear misfortune everywhere with me, let
it at least be kept far from thee." " Ah!
remain," she replies, quickly, " misfortune
can do nothing where despair already
reigns," and while once more they con-
template each other in silence, overcome
by growing emotion, Hunding, the stern
husband, the savage warrior, his helmet
bristling with curious ornaments, shows
himself on the threshold. " It is a guest,
worn out with fatigue, who demands shel-
ter," says Siglinda, answering her hus-
band's look of inquiry. " Hospitality is.
sacred to me," says Hunding to the un-
known; " may my house be sacred to
thee," and with a gesture he orders the
repast. Sigmund then relates from whence
he is come. Vanquished in a combat with

a neighboring chief, stripped of his arms, he was obliged to flee through the tempest. "Thou makest light of misfortune," cries Hunding; "the chief whom thou hast just named is my ally; thus hast thou chanced upon thy own mortal enemy. I accord thee shelter beneath my roof, however, until morning; afterward, out of my house, and let us meet in combat." And Hunding retires with a sombre mien, dragging with him Siglinda, who casts a despairing glance at the unfortunate guest.

Sigmund, spent with fatigue, falls again by the fireside, insensible. Where may he find strength with which to defend himself? Who will come to his aid in this bitter distress? Siglinda reappears. She has poured out the juices of a sleep-making plant for her husband. The stranger will be saved, provided he can wrench from the tree's trunk a marvellous sword, which an old man once thrust into it. Truly the sword is destined for Sigmund, for it yields at his first effort. Behold, it glistens in his hand. Henceforward he fears nothing. He will be able to defend the beloved woman, whom now he recognizes. Is she not his twin sister, formerly carried off from the devastated fireside? He will find her again, and wrest her from the enemy. "My love! my sister!" he cries, passionately. And folding her in his arms, he bears her from the sad dwelling through the moonlit forest.

In the second act we see again the mountains inhabited by the gods. Wotan joyously announces to Brunhild, the beautiful Walkyria, armed with silver helmet and cuirass, that to-day she must award the victory to Sigmund, the beloved hero of the gods. But while the happy Walkyria utters her war-cry, and bounds from summit to summit on her black horse, Fricka, the jealous goddess, protector of conjugal vows, arrives in her chariot, drawn by rams. She demands vengeance for the outraged Hunding. "This Sigmund whom thou protectest," she says, "is not the free hero who should redeem thee, for thou hast guided him, pushed him to this end. Sigmund must die." Wotan is overcome. The goddess is right. Sigmund has not acted by his own free-will. He must then abandon this unfortunate youth. The god, overpowered with grief, comes, however, to this conclusion. The hero, doomed to perish, must be conducted by the Walkyria to Walhalla. Here come the fugitives, pursued by the infuriated Hunding. Siglinda, at the end of her endurance, swoons in the arms of her fraternal lover. It is then that the saddened Walkyria shows herself to Sigmund. "Who art thou," he says, "who appearest to me so beautiful and so grave?" "Those who behold me have only a few hours to live," she replies. "Soon thou wilt follow me to the dwelling of the gods." "And Sig-

linda, will she come also?" he asks. "No;
she must still live on earth." "Then thou
deceivest thyself; I will not be separated
from her, for we will both die here." And
he raises his sword over Siglinda.

In the face of this love and sorrow, the
Walkyria for the first time feels herself
moved by a human emotion. "Stay!"
she cries, go without fear to the contest;
I shall protect thee." Soon the savage
Hunding shouts his defiance to Sigmund;
the adversaries meet in battle upon a sum-
mit half lost in the clouds. Hunding is
on the point of triumph; but the Walkyria
appears in a light, and covers Sigmund
with her buckler. Wotan, irritated by
Brunhild's disobedience, shows himself
also in a storm-cloud, and setting loose
the lightning, shatters the sword in the
hands of Sigmund, who falls mortally
wounded.

The third act shows a rugged rock upon
which Brunhild's sisters, the Walkyrias,

reunite after the combat. Here they come
in haste, riding through the clouds illumin-
ated by the lightning; they call to one
another joyously, with savage cries, strik-
ing their arms tumultuously. But Brun-
hild arrives all tearful; she has brought
in her arms Siglinda, who does not wish
to survive her lover. "Live!" she says
to her, "live for the brave hero whom
thou bearest in thy bosom." And she
gives her the precious fragments of Sig-
mund's sword. "Save her, my sisters,
save the poor woman," she adds; "for
myself I must remain here to suffer the
punishment of my fault." In fact, Wotan's
voice resounds, full of anger. He soon
rejoins the guilty goddess who has
violated the supreme command. "I
obeyed not thy order, but thy secret
wish," says Brunhild. The god, alas! is
not free, primordial laws enchain him;
he cannot pardon. The fallen Walkyria
must sleep upon the road at the mercy of

the first comer who will find her. "So be it," she says; "but surround me with a sea of flames that he who will approach must at least be a hero. With what sadness does the god separate from his dearly-loved one, and take her divinity from her in a supreme kiss! She is now only a sleeping woman, around whom a flaming rampart is lighted.

SECOND DAY: SIGFRID.

AFTER Sigmund's death Siglinda, having taken refuge in a wild forest, gave birth to a son, and died, confiding him to the Nibelung, Mime, whom Alberich, first possessor of the gold, had formerly forced to forge the all-powerful ring. The deformed dwarf had brought up the descendant of the gods in his cave, not in the spirit of devotion, but with the sole idea of making him of service later in the conquest of the gold, the object of all desires. Sigfrid is now a handsome youth, im-

petuous and uncontrollable, whose heroic
spirits are awaking, and who dreams of
conquering the world.   Meanwhile he
reigns master of the forest; the joyous
sound of his silver horn replies to the
birds' songs; the young madcap bounds
with the roe and overthrows the deer.
There he comes rushing into the cavern;
his pealing laugh resounds.   He drags
after him, to Mime's terror, a black bear,
which he has just got into his posses-
sion.

But these sports and contests satisfy
him no longer.   Impatiently he questions
the dwarf in regard to the world, to him
unknown; he wishes to get away, leave
the forest never to return.   Mime then
shows him the fragments of the sword
shattered by the lightning in Sigmund's
hands.   Siglinda has bequeathed it to her
son as the most precious of inheritances.
Sigfrid takes possession of these fragments
of steel, lights the forge fire, and throws

the pieces into the crucible. Then rais-
ing the heavy hammer with a triumphal
song he completely reforges Wotan's
sword. He soon brandishes it, still smok-
ing, and with a single blow he cleaves in
two the anvil, henceforward useless.

Mime then conducts the young hero to
the wildest part of the forest, before the
cave where the giant Fafner, in the form of
a dragon, guards the gold wrested from the
Nibelung. Sigfrid, laughing all the while
at his hideous aspect, fights with and kills
the monster. He disdains the treasure,
taking only the ring, of whose power he is
ignorant, and a magic helmet which per-
mits the wearer to assume any form. The
young man, as if weary, throws himself at
the foot of a tree all bathed in sunlight;
he listens dreamily to the thousand rust-
lings of the forest. An unknown desire
stirs his heart. While the birds fly in
couples he is alone. He thinks of his
mother, of this mysterious being, man's

companion, whom he has never seen, and of whom he knows nothing. The song of a bird flying over his head finally captivates his attention. He listens; he seems to comprehend the meaning of this song. The bird speaks to him. May it not be his mother's soul? " Ah, Sigfrid," it says, " now thou possessest the treasure, thou should'st conquer the most beautiful of women. She sleeps upon a high rock, surrounded by flames; but shouldst thou dare to pass through the furnace, the warlike virgin would be thine." And Sigfrid, filled with enthusiasm, follows the bird, which takes its flight as if to guide him toward the lovely bride.

In the third act we see Wotan again. Leaning over the brink of a gulf, in gloomy anguish, he invokes Erda, the lurid goddess who sees the world's destinies; he will question her once again in regard to this fall of the gods, which she has announced to him. At this sovereign voice the sleeper rouses herself; with half-closed eyes she slowly rises from the abyss, wrapped in her dull veils, and covered with dew. But she has no further information to give to Wotan. The end is inevitable. As if submerged by their own creation the gods will become effaced before men. "So be it," cries Wotan, wearied perhaps of his divinity; "it is to this end that I aspire." However, when Sigfrid, leaping from rock to rock, his eyes fixed upon his winged guide, passes near Wotan, this latter tries to bar his way; but the free and fearless hero breaks the god's lance with a single blow of the sword which, without assistance, he has forged for himself. Then he rushes joyously to the assault of the burning rampart, passes fearlessly through the furnace, beholds at last the sleeping warrior in her silver cuirass; and, all quivering with love, awakens her with a kiss.

THIRD DAY: GLOOM OF THE GODS.

UNDER the nocturnal shade of an ash as old as the world itself the three Fates spin and weave men's destinies. Their cold gaze is plunged into the future, where they see only distress and malediction. They throw from one to the other the thread which they have been spinning uninterruptedly from the beginning of time. But suddenly the thread snaps in their hands; the sombre spinners, seized with fear, press closely together, and descend to the depths of the earth to take refuge near the wise Erda. Then day breaks. Sigfrid and Brunhilda, supporting one another, come out of the mysterious grotto which shelters their happiness. The goddess has divested herself of her divinity for her dearly-loved hero; she has unveiled to him the mysteries of the sacred ruins and the knowledge of the gods; but it now appears to her that she has given

nothing to him who has revealed love to
her. It is necessary that Sigfrid should
leave her for a time, and that he should
go in search of new exploits. It is he
who thenceforward will wear the Wal-
kyria's armor, and bound upon the savage
courser who formerly sped with the storm.
Before his departure the hero gives to
Brunhilda the gold ring, which to the
lovers is only a pledge of fidelity, and they
part after taking a mutual oath of eternal
love.

In his adventurous course through the
world, Sigfrid arrives at the dwelling of
Gunter, a powerful chief on the Rhinish
borders. Gutrune, his lovely sister, lives
with this warrior, also the sinister Hagen,
whom Alberich, the Nibelung, has begot-
ten of a woman whom he misled by the
attraction of the gold. The Nibelung has
bequeathed his hatred toward the offspring
of the gods to his son, and has charged
him to regain the all-powerful ring.

Hagen is already plotting Sigfrid's ruin, when this latter crosses the threshold, with joyous impetuosity, crying to Gunter, " Fight with me, or let us be friends!" The chief receives him amicably, and Gutrune, advised by Hagen, pours out for him a fatal draught, which will disturb his mind to such a degree as to efface all remembrance. The young girl's resplendent eyes complete his infatuation, and he soon forgets Brunhilda and her love; his new passion has obliterated everything, and he demands his host's sister in marriage. "Give her to him," breathes Hagen to Gunter, " on condition that he shall go and conquer for thee the marvellous woman sleeping in the midst of the flames." Brunhilda's name makes no impression upon Sigfrid's soul; he remembers no longer. Certainly he will go without delay to the conquest of this bride for his brother-in-arms, and without tarrying further, he takes his departure, impatient to return.

Soon the fallen goddess, crushed and
stupefied, is brought to Gunter. Sigfrid,
after wresting from her the ring, symbol
of constant tenderness, has dragged her by
force to deliver her over to a stranger,
while he now hastens into the arms of
another woman. As the love of the
daughter of the gods was sublime and ab-
solute, so is her anger terrible in the face
of this betrayal. Sigfrid is doomed to
death. It is only by death that Brunhilda
can reconquer the radiant hero to whom
she has given all. He is destined to per-
ish at the hunt, treacherously struck.
The daughters of the Rhine emerge from
the waves to warn him, at the same time
demanding from him the ring, which en-
velopes him with its malediction; but Sig-
frid refuses to restore it to them. Soon
after, while he is giving his companions a
recital of his life, seeing again little by
little the thread of his memory, Hagen sud-
denly and treacherously strikes him with

his lance. The hero sinks to the earth
and dies, pronouncing the name, once
more recalled, of Brunhilda. The war-
riors, in consternation, lay Sigfrid's body
upon his buckler, and carry him slowly
away in the light of the pale rising moon.

In the last scene a groaning crowd
bears Sigfrid's body under the massive
portals of Gunter's dwelling, gloomily
lighted by torches, and mingles its lament
with the dull roar of the Rhine, whose
dark waves flow in the background.
Gutrune bursts into tears of despair, but
Brunhilda, solemnly advancing, puts an
end to this clamor. "I have heard," she
says, "the tears of children lamenting
their mother, but no lament worthy of a
hero." Then she commands a vast
funeral pile to be built, and when it has
been lighted with a torch, and Sigfrid
laid upon it, contemplating him with in-
describable emotion, she withdraws from
his finger the fatal ring, the cause of all

misfortunes. "Suffering has made me prophetic," she says: "those who should efface the fault of the gods are predestined to misfortune and death. May our sacrifice put an end to the curse. May the ring be purified by fire. May the waters dissolve it forever! The end of the gods is at hand. But if I leave the world without a master, I bequeath to men the most sublime treasure in my knowledge. Know, then, that neither gold, nor divine splendor, nor omnipotence, gives happiness. Happiness, in joy or in suffering, comes from love alone." She has her horse brought to her by a Walkyria, and, leaping into the saddle, with one bound she rushes into the furnace. Then the Rhine overflows tumultuously, dispersing the ashes of the funeral pile. The daughters of the Rhine joyously lift up the reconquered ring, while Hagen, who had rushed forward to seize it again, is carried away with the flood, and on the heights in a dim light the Walhalla is seen crumbling about the gods, who fade away, and become effaced.

PARSIFAL: A LYRICAL FEAST.

FIRST ACT.

THE first act of Parsifal takes us to Mont Salvat, in the country where the mysterious temple of the Grail rises upon the northern side of the mountains of the Spanish Visigoths. A magnificent forest glade, on the border of a beautiful lake, is just waking in the first gleam of dawn. Two youthful shield-bearers and Gurnemanz, a robust old man, are sleeping, stretched upon the grass at the foot of a tree. From the further side of the temple and castle, which are not seen, is heard the sound of trumpets solemnly pealing forth the early morning summons, and the

sleepers, whose mission it is to watch over
the sacred forest, start up ashamed of
having allowed themselves to be overcome
by sleep. Gurnemanz gently reproves
the young men; then all three prostrate
themselves in silent prayer. The old man
is the first to rise. "Up now, youths," he
cries, "the hour is come for attending
upon the king; already I see messengers
coming toward us preceding the bed of
pain which supports him." And ap-
proaching two knights who descend from
the castle he cries: "Greetings to you:
how does Amfortas find himself to-day?
Truly he descends early toward the waters
of the lake; tell me, the healing plant
obtained for him by Gawan's skill and
audacity has, I presume, brought him
relief?"

"Thou presumest, thou who knowest
all," replies the knight. "His sufferings
soon returned more heavy than ever, and
deprived of sleep by the violence of the

pain, the king eagerly called for his bath."

" Fools that we are to hope for relief, where only recovery can heal!" murmurs Gurnemanz, sadly bending his head. "Seek every herb, every philter, wander over the entire earth! For him there is only one help, one saviour!" But the old man returns an evasive answer to the knight who demands this saviour's name. The shield-bearers, who have withdrawn and look toward the valley at the rear of the scene, suddenly perceive a strange, savage woman upon a running horse, which seems to fly over the fields. Soon, bounding from her saddle, she precipitates herself impetuously upon the scene. Her black hair falls half-plaited upon a forehead of bronzen pallor; her shining eyes are sad and fixed; her savage dress is held by a girdle of serpents' skins. "Hold," she says to Gurnemanz, "take this balm; if it heal not, Arabia contains nothing that can

help the king. Question me not, I am
weary." And she throws herself upon the
ground like an exhausted animal. This
woman is the savage and mysterious Kun-
dry. No one knows who she is, nor from
whence she comes. She has constituted
herself messenger to the Knights of the
Grail. She accomplishes the most perilous
missions with skill and zeal, but never does
she accept thanks; her ironic laughter and
her sinister glance seem to belie the good
she does. A frightful curse seems to
weigh upon her. Sometimes she disap-
pears for months, and Gurnemanz has
often found her worn out under a bush,
plunged in a strange, deathlike sleep.

A procession of shield-bearers and
knights precede Amfortas, borne upon a
litter. They stop for a moment, and the
king lets his feverish glance wander over
the wholesome freshness of the woods.
"Ah!" he murmurs, "after the exaspera-
tion of this painful night, behold the mag-

nificent early dawn of the forest; the
waters of the sacred lake will revive me,
pain will cease, and the chaos of suffer-
ing will clear away. Gawan!" "Gawan,
my king, is no longer here; the virtue of
this dearly-acquired plant, having disap-
pointed thy hope, he has taken his flight
toward new researches." "Without my
permission!" cries the king. "Let him
expiate this infraction of the Grail's laws!
Oh, woe to him, rash, self-willed, if he
fall into Klingsor's snares. Let nothing
further trouble our peace. I wait for that
which is destined for me." "Knowing
by compassion, was it not thus?" "It is
thus that thou hast told us." "A harm-
less fool only; I think I recognize him.
Ah, I should call him Death!" "But
make yet a trial of this," says Gurne-
manz, holding toward him the phial
brought by Kundry. "From whence
came this mysterious phial?" demanded
the king.

" It is brought to thee from Arabia."

" And who obtained it? "

" She who lies yonder; the savage woman. Rise, Kundry, come hither." But Kundry refuses to stir.

" It is thou," says Amfortas. " Must I again thank thee, indefatigable and unknown maid? So be it; I will yet try this balm, were it only out of gratitude for thy fidelity."

But, agitated, Kundry says: "No thanks! Ha! Ha! Of what good is this balm? No thanks! Away! Go to thy bath!" And while the procession moves away, and Gurnemanz sadly follows the king with a heavy glance, the shield-bearers scoff at Kundry who lies stretched upon the ground like a beast of the forest; but Gurnemanz defends her, and reprimands the youths, recalling the services which she has never ceased to render to them. "And yet she hates us," says one of them. " See how she sneers as she looks at us."

"She is a pagan, a sorceress."

"Yes," says Gurnemanz, "she well may be a damned soul. Perhaps she lives now incarnate to expiate the sins of a former life, sins which are not yet pardoned. If her repentance disposes her to acts profitable to our order, she serves us, and purchases back her own redemption."

"If she be truly faithful and intrepid," says one of the shield-bearers, "send her to reconquer the lost lance."

"That is a work forbidden to all," cries Gurnemanz, in gloom, and adds with emotion: "O source of wounds! O source of miracles! Sacred lance! I see thee brandished by the most sacrilegious hand! Too audacious Amfortas, who could'st have restrained thyself when armed with this lance, thou resolvedst to attack the magician? Already, on the confines of the enemy's castle, the hero is taken from us. . . . A woman of terrifying beauty has subjugated him. Filled

with love he is in her arms. The sacred
lance falls from his hand. A cry of death!
I fly toward the king! Klingsor disap-
pears with a sneer. He has stolen the
divine lance. Fighting, I protect the king's
flight. But a wound burns in his side. It
is this selfsame wound that will not
heal."

The shield-bearers have come and
seated themselves in a listening attitude
at the old man's feet. "Dear father,"
they say, "speak again. Tell us thou
hast known Klingsor? How is that?"
"Listen," says Gurnemanz: "Titurel
knew him well. It was at the time when
the cunning and strength of savage
enemies menaced the kingdom of the pure
faith that in a solemn and sacred night
our king, the holy hero Titurel, saw
bending toward him the blessed mes-
senger of the Redeemer. The chalice
from which he drank at the time of the
Lord's Supper, this cup of august and

sacred election, which later, when he was
upon the cross, received his divine blood,
together with this selfsame lance which
caused his blood to gush forth, — these
most precious among the sacred relics,
were confided to the safekeeping of
our king by the celestial messengers.
Then Titurel erected the sanctuary. You,
who have attained to his service by paths
inaccessible to sinners, know that only
pure men are permitted to associate them-
selves with these brethren, consecrated to
the highest works of deliverance, and for-
tified by the sacred and miraculous virtue
of the Grail. This is why he, in regard
to whom you question me, Klingsor, re-
mained excluded, notwithstanding all his
pains. Beyond the mountains, in the
valley, he became a hermit; all around
stretched the luxuriant land of the
infidels. What sin he had committed
yonder, remained hidden from me; but he
desiréd expiation; he aspired even to

sanctity. Powerless to destroy his guilty
desires, he laid a criminal hand upon him-
self. That hand, which he stretched out
toward the Grail, was repulsed with scorn
by its guardians. Rage then taught
Klingsor how the horrible crime of his
sacrifice could serve him to exercise a
fatal charm; he changed his desert into a
garden of delight. There, growing like
flowers, are seductively beautiful women,
who, by their infernal fascinations, endeavor
to attract the Knights of the Grail. He
who yields to this seduction is made his
own, and already, alas! many are lost to
us. When Titurel, bowed down by age,
confided the kingdom to his son, Amfortas,
this latter would take no rest until he had
done away with this scourge of hell. You
know what happened. The lance is in
Klingsor's hands, and as, by its virtue, he
can wound even the saints, he imagines
that he has already taken the Grail from
us."

"Ah! before all else, the lance must be restored to us," cries a shield-bearer.

"Happiness and honor to him who will restore it."

And Gurnemanz resumes: "Amfortas, prostrated in ardent prayer before the deserted shrine, implored a sign of deliverance, when a gentle light emanated from the Grail, and a holy apparition spoke to him distinctly, and he clearly discerned these words: 'Let a harmless fool only, knowing by compassion, await him whom I have chosen.'"

But while the shield-bearers repeat the words of the oracle with profound emotion, cries resound in the forest.

"Misfortune! misfortune! who is the criminal?"

"What is it?" ask Gurnemanz and the shield-bearers.

"Yonder! . . . a swan! . . . a wild swan! . . . he is wounded!"

"Who wounded it?"

Two knights, arriving unexpectedly, reply, —

" The king greeted the bird's whirling flight over the lake as a happy omen, when an arrow was let fly."

New shield-bearers bring Parsifal forward and say: "Look! here is he who sent the arrow."

" Is it thou who hast killed the swan?" demands Gurnemanz.

" Truly," cries Parsifal, " I shoot upon the wing whatever flies."

" Unprecedented misdeed! thou hast then committed a murder here in this sacred wood, whose peacefulness surrounded thee; did not the familiar beasts approach thee, gentle and caressing? What had this faithful swan done to thee? To us it was a friend. What is it now to thee? Behold the snowy plumage stained with blood, the drooping wings, the dying glance, — Dost thou recognize thy fault?"

"I did not know," says Parsifal, greatly troubled. And he breaks his bow with violence.

They question him: "From whence dost thou come? What is thy name? Who has sent thee?"

The young man knows nothing of all this; he knows not even if he have a name. But Kundry, who has fixed an eager glance upon Parsifal, answers for him: "His mother brought him an orphan into the world, when Gamuret was slain in combat. To preserve her son from a hero's premature death she brought him up in the forest, a stranger to arms, like a fool, the mad woman."

"Yes," says Parsifal, who has listened with lively attention, "and once glittering men, mounted upon beautiful animals, passed along the borders of the forest. I wished to resemble them, but they laughed at me, and passed rapidly by. Then I ran after them, but I could not overtake them.

I came to wild places upon mountains, in valleys; often night fell, the day returned; my bow defended me against the deer and the giants."

"Yes," cries Kundry, eagerly, "the evil-doers and giants were overcome by his strength. They all fear the valiant youth " —

"Who fears me, say?"

"The wicked."

"Were those who menaced me wicked? Who is good?"

"Thy mother, from whom thou hast escaped," says Gurnemanz; "she weeps and grieves for thy sake."

"Her grief is over; his mother is dead," says Kundry.

"Dead! my mother! who says that?" cries Parsifal, throwing himself furiously upon Kundry, and seizing her by the throat.

"Violence again, mad youth!" says Gurnemanz, holding him back.

"I perish," cries the young man, stag-
gering. Kundry has rushed ₄toward a
forest stream, and comes to bathe Parsifal's
forehead with fresh water.

"It is well thus," says the old man,
"such is the grace of the Grail, you banish
evil when you do great good."

But Kundry turns sadly away. "I
never do good," she murmurs, "I seek
only repose. Alas! repose for her who is
wretched. Ah! horror seizes me, resist-
ance is vain, the time is come, sleep, sleep
I must." And with a stifled cry, she sinks
down behind a bush. Gurnemanz, how-
ever, hoping that this may be the redeemer
promised to the king, conducts Parsifal
toward the temple; he will be present at
the ceremony, and should Parsifal be the
chosen one, his mission will be revealed to
him by the Grail.

The scene changes; the forest dis-
appears, while the old man and Parsifal
appear to be advancing; the side of a

large rock conceals them, then they re-
appear in the galleries. Sounds of trum-
pets gently swell forth, and bells toll
louder and louder. They finally arrive
in a vast hall, whose lofty cupola permits
the daylight to penetrate like a luminous
flood. The Knights of the Grail, clad in
the white coat-of-arms, a dove embroid-
ered upon their mantle, advance in two
lines and chant piously: "Each day pre-
pared for love's last repast, and troubling
himself little that it may be perhaps for
the last time, may it strengthen to-day
him who can rejoice in his acts, and may
the repast be renewed unto him. Let
him approach the holy table and receive
the divine gift." Voices of youths re-
spond from the halls and heights: "As
formerly, with a thousand pains, his blood
flowed for sinning humanity, may my
blood be poured out with a joyous heart
for the hero Saviour, and may this body
which he has offered for our redemption

live in us by his death." And children's
voices answer back from the cupola's
very heights: "Faith lives, the dove soars,
sweet messenger of the Saviour; drink of
the wine which flows for you, and eat of
the bread of life."

Shield-bearers and serving-brothers then
enter, bearing the litter upon which Am-
fortas lies. Children advance, bearing a
shrine covered with a scarlet cloth, which
they proceed to place upon a marble altar.
Suddenly from a vaulted niche at the end
of the hall behind the altar a voice makes
itself·heard. It is that of the aged Titurel.
" My son, Amfortas," he says, " doest thou
officiate? Must I behold the Grail yet
again to-day and live? Must I die, no
longer sustained by my Saviour?"

" Alas! alas! oh, grievous sorrow!"
cries Amfortas. " My father, perform once
more thy holy office. Oh, live, and let me
die." And Titurel: " I live in the tomb
by the grace of our Lord, but I am too

feeble to serve him. Expiate thou thy
sin in his service. Uncover the Grail."

"No, uncover it not," cries Amfortas, in
a passion of despair. "Oh! can no one
measure the torment which the sight that
transports you awakens in me? What is
the wound and its agony of pain com-
pared with the infernal suffering of being
damned here to officiate? Oh, sorrowful
heritage which has fallen to me! I must
guard the sublimest of sanctuaries, I, the
only sinner among you all! Oh, chastise-
ment, chastisement without equal, inflicted
by the all-merciful One whom I have
offended! Alas! to him and to the mercy
of his salvation I ardently aspire from the
depths of my soul; by expiatory penitence
I hope to return to him. The hour ap-
proaches, a ray of light descends upon the
sacred work, the veil falls, the sacred cup
is illumined with a radiant lustre; over-
come by the celestial possession of pain,
I feel the stream of divine blood flowing

through my heart, and the impure wave of my own blood rushes impetuously back in wild terror to cast itself toward the world of lust; it breaks anew its bonds, and gushes from the wound, like unto his, made by the lance which of yore opened in the Redeemer's side this wound which weeps in pity's sacred ardor tears of blood for the world's iniquity! And from this wound flows, though I be the keeper of divinest treasures, of the redeeming balm, the fiery blood, renewed without respite by the fountain of longing, which, alas! no penitence can extinguish. Mercy, mercy! oh, all-merciful one. Ah! in pity take from me my heritage, close the wound that I may die purified, and be born again in holiness unto thee."

As the king sinks down exhausted the knights murmur in a low tone: "Let a harmless fool only, knowing by compassion, await him — him whom I have chosen. Such is the revelation; await

with hope, and this day officiate." "Un-
cover the Grail," exclaims Titurel. The
king has raised himself in silence, he
opens the golden shrine, and draws from
it the ancient relic, the crystal cup in
which Joseph of Arimathea received the
blood of Christ; it is the miraculous
Grail! A twilight dimness has invaded
the hall, a single ray coming from above
falls upon the Grail, and illumines it with
a constantly-growing glory. From the
cupola's heights children's voices are
heard: "Take my blood in the name of
our love! Take my body in remembrance
of me."

They add: "By compassion and love
the Saviour once changed the bread and
wine of the supreme repast into the blood
which he has shed, and the body which
he has sacrificed. The blood and flesh of
the sacrifice the Redeemer whom you
glorify changes to-day into this wine
which flows for you and this bread which
you eat."

Then the knights: "Take the bread, transform it without fear into strength and valor of body. Faithful even unto death, intrepid in suffering, accomplish the Saviour's works. Take this wine, transform it anew into life's burning blood, to fight, united in fraternal fidelity, with joyous courage." All rise and exchange the kiss of peace. And the voices from above cry: "Blessed in the faith! Blessed in love! Blessed in love! Blessed in the faith!"

Parsifal has watched this scene with haggard eyes; but it has only left his mind in a profound stupor. Gurnemanz, disappointed in his hope, takes him by the arm and says: "Go, take thy way thither. Thou art but a harmless fool. But Gurnemanz counsels thee for thy future to leave the swans in peace. Seek rather after geese, thou gosling." He pushes Parsifal out, slams the door, and while he follows the knights the curtain descends.

SECOND ACT.

In the second act we find ourselves in the castle of the magician Klingsor, situate upon the confines of Spanish Arabia. The scene represents the empty interior of an embattled tower. Along the walls narrow steps only project, ascending toward the battlements, or flat ledges of rocks. Klingsor, the enchanter, is seated upon one of these before a metallic mirror; he gazes intently into its depths, and in its magic shadows sees Parsifal advancing, joyous and thoughtless, drawn by a charm toward the enchanted castle. Klingsor well knows that this is the redeemer promised to the King of the Grail; if, however, the magician can succeed in drawing him into the snares of the flesh before the young madcap will have realized the high mission for which he is chosen, Amfortas's safety is at an end. Klingsor will employ all his cunning and the most pow-

erful seductions to ruin the pure and art-
less youth. Leaning over the tower's
gloomy depths, he burns aromatics, whose
smoke ascends in bluish clouds; then, with
mysterious gestures, he pronounces a for-
mula of incantation: "Come hither! obey
thy master, rouse thyself at his call, thou,
the nameless and primeval devil, rose of
hell who wast formerly Herodias; rise,
rise toward thy master, obey him who
holds thee in absolute control."

Kundry appears, slowly rising from the
shadows. Like a creature rudely awak-
ened from a profound sleep, she utters a
horrible cry of fear, which little by little
becomes extinguished in a feeble moan of
distress. It is she, it is the power of her
beauty which should cause the ingenious
youth to fall into the magicians' power.
Is it not in her arms that the King of the
Grail forgot his holy duties? Is it not on
her account that he now suffers and writhes
in the cruel flame of guilty desire? In

vain the temptress struggles and attempts
to escape from the power which holds
her in dominion; the impure fires which
burn within her will force her to yield.
Good and evil tumultuously dispute the
possession of this soul, already several
times incarnate. Like a feminine Ahas-
uerus, she formerly insulted Christ, and is
condemned to be born again ceaselessly
in sin's suffering. In vain she aspires to
deliverance, she inevitably falls back again
into the snares of the flesh. He who
would resist the enchantress might per-
haps save her; but before her beauty all
are weak, all damn themselves with her.
He, Klingsor, holds her in his power, and
knows how to rouse her from the lethar-
gic sleep, into which he plunges her at
will.

"For me alone, thy seductions are
powerless," he says to her.

"Ah! ah!" she cries with a harsh
laugh, "would'st thou be chaste?"

"What dost thou ask, cursed woman?" shrieks Klingsor in a rage. "Oh, cruel torment! It is thus that Satan scoffs me because I formerly struggled for holiness; cruel torment, torment of unsubdued desire, hellish urgency of horrible instincts, upon which I have imposed the silence of death. Does he laugh now, and does he jeer at me by thy mouth, thou bride of the devil? Beware, such scorn and raillery one has expiated already, — he who once cast me from him, proud in the strength of his sanctity; his race is to-day in my power, and the guardian of the holy of holies must languish unredeemed. Soon, I think, I shall myself watch over the Grail! Ha! ha! he pleased thee, this Amfortas, the hero whom I assigned to thee for thy joy."

"Oh, woe! woe!" groans Kundry, "he also weak, all are weak, all have fallen with me by my damnation. Oh, eternal sleep, thou only blessing, how attain thee?"

"Ah! he who would resist thee would deliver thee; make thy trial upon the youth who approaches."

Kundry struggles already more feebly. "He is handsome, this youth," exclaims Klingsor, who looks from the castle's height; see, he mounts toward the castle. Hey, hey! Guardians! Knights! Heralds! About! The enemy approaches. Ah! how they defend the walls, the egotistical fools, to protect their gracious devils! That is it. Courage, courage! Ho! ho! this one has no fear; he has just snatched his lance from the hero Ferris. He brandishes it intrepidly toward the horde of combatants. How little their zeal serves them, the dullards! The child breaks the arm of one, the thigh of another. Ha! ha! they draw back, they take flight, each carrying away a wound. Thus am I happy! Thus may the entire race of

knights cut one another's throats! Ah!
thou tender shoot; although omens may
have forwarned thee, yet art thou fallen
into my power, too young, too innocent,
— thy purity once stained, thou art mine."

Kundry, seized as if in spite of herself
with a fit of ecstatic laughter, has disap-
peared. The tower sinks little by little,
and in its place one sees a marvellous
garden filled with a tropical vegetation,
beyond which appear the terraces and
porticos of an Arabian palace of the most
sumptuous style. Parsifal advances, stu-
pefied with surprise, in the midst of all
this splendor; ravishing young girls, simi-
lar to living flowers, at first alarmed, but
soon becoming reassured, press about him,
completing the measure of his stupefac-
tion by all the charms and graces which
they display for his enchantment and ruin.
"If thou art gracious to us hold not thy-
self at a distance," they say, "and if thou
wilt not quarrel with us we will recom-

pense thee. We do not play for gold, our
only stake is love. If thou thinkest to
console us, surely thou wilt gain it. Come,
come, gentle youth, let us bloom for thee.
Our loving caresses are intended for
thee."

"What fragrant perfume you exhale,"·
says Parsifal, with tranquil gayety; "are
you flowers?"

"Beauties of this garden, fragrant spirits,
in the springtime the master gathers us!
We grow here in the summer sunlight,
and bloom joyously for thee. Be thou
then gracious and friendly to us, accord
to the flowers thy sweet tribute. If thou
wilt not love us, we shall wither and die."

"Take me upon thy breast."

"Let me refresh thy forehead."

"Let me kiss thy mouth."

"No, I . . . I am the fairest."

"No, my perfume's the sweetest."

But Parsifal laughingly repulses them:
"You, medley of flowers, gracious and

wild," he says, "if you wish me to share in your sports widen this narrow circle."

"Why dost thou chide?"

"Because you are in conflict."

"We struggle for thy love."

"Do not struggle."

"Go. He wants me."

"No, he desires me."

"Dost thou repel me?".

"Art thou timid in the presence of women?"

"Thou lettest the flowers court the butterfly."

"Leave me, you will not catch me," exclaims the young man, who would take flight.

Then Kundry appears voluptuously stretched upon a bed of flowers. She is of supreme beauty, and adorned in the strangest and most superb manner in the oriental fashion. "Parsifal, stay," she cries. At the sound of this voice the young girls, frightened, withdraw regretfully, casting tender glances toward the handsome youth. "All hail to thee, thou innocent fool!" And they disappear with stifled laughter.

"Parsifal!" . . . murmurs the young man, stupefied, "my mother once called me thus in a dream." Then, with the majesty of a goddess, and the tenderness of love, the seducer speaks to him of the mother whom he abandoned, and who died after long tortures of despair. "My mother! my mother! can I have forgotten her," exclaims Parsifal. "Alas! alas! what have I ever remembered? A crushing madness alone possesses me!" And overpowered with grief, he sinks at Kundry's feet. "Confession and repentance will blot out thy sin," she says, bending toward him; "they will change folly to reason; learn to understand the love which enveloped Gamuret when influenced by thy mother's passion. The love that gave thee form and existence, before

which death and madness must draw back,
gives thee to-day, with the supreme greet-
ing of the maternal benediction, its first
kiss." And with a most radiant smile,
the enchantress leans over the young man
and presses a long kiss upon his mouth.
At the contact of their lips Parsifal rises
quickly, as if transfigured; the veil which
enveloped his mind is suddenly torn away;
he now comprehends the meaning of
everything he has seen; he feels kindling
in his own heart the devouring fire with
which Amfortas burns. "The wound!
the wound!" he cries, "it burns in my
heart. Oh, lamentation! frightful lamen-
tation! it cries out from the very depths
of my being. Here, here in the heart is
the flame, the burning desire, the terrible
and unbidden desire which seizes all my
senses and subjugates them! Oh, tor-
ment of love! how the whole framework
shudders, trembles, and thrills with guilty
desires!"

Again he sees Amfortas before the Grail, and the horror of sacrilege, the sinner's torture he now understands.

"Superb hero, fly the illusion, be gracious at the approach of grace," says the temptress, filled with passionate admiration. And he, still prostrated at her feet, regards her fixedly while she displays before him all the charms of her beauty. "Yes," he says, "this voice! it is thus that she called him, and this glance which smiled upon him, I recognize it! These lips, yes, it is thus that he saw them quiver, it is thus that she bent her head, thus raised it proudly. In this manner flowed her silken curls, thus she enfolded him and gently caressed his cheek. Allied to all the tortures of suffering, she kissed away from him his soul's salvation. Ah! such kisses!" Raising himself quickly he repulses Kundry impetuously.

"Away, corrupter!" he cries, "far from me forever."

The lofty mission which he is destined
to accomplish is now revealed to him; he
must defy, like Amfortas, all the pleas-
ures of guilty temptations, suffer all that
he has suffered; but resist where he has
yielded, and triumph where the other has
succumbed; this is the price by which he
will save him.

Kundry, in a delirium of furious passion,
sets loose in vain all the seductions of
hell against him; in vain she endeavors
to soften him: "Ah cruel one, if thou
feelest naught in thy heart but the suffer-
ings of others, feel also mine. If thou be
the Saviour, why not unite thyself to me
for my salvation; during eternities I have
awaited thee. Oh! if thou couldst know
the curse which sleeping and waking
in torment and laughter invigorates me
endlessly for new suffering. I saw Him,
Him, and I laughed. His glance fell upon
me. Since then I seek this glance from
world to world, I shall meet it again yet;

in the height of my distress I seem to see it, I feel it resting upon me. Then the cursed laughter seizes me again. A sinner falls into my arms, and I laugh, I laugh; I cannot weep. I can only cry out, carried deliriously into the night of folly ever renewed, from which penitence itself scarce arouses me. Him whom I ardently desire in the midst of my agony I recognize in thee; let me weep upon thy breast and unite myself to thee for a single hour, and though seemingly rejected by God and the world, let me be saved and redeemed in thee."

"Thou wouldst be damned with me for all eternity if for one hour I should forget my mission in the embrace of thy arms."

. . . "It was my kiss which rendered thy eyes clear? the full gift of my love would give thee divinity. Save the world if that is thy mission, and if this hour has made thee a god, let me suffer damnation forever. Only give me thy love."

"Thee too will I save, sinner; show me but the road which I have lost, the way which leads to Amfortas."

"Never, never! thou shalt not find him," cries Kundry, transported with rage. "Error, imposition, illusion, bar his way, entangle the paths that his feet may never enter upon the road which he seeks; may all ways be cursed that estrange him from me. Aberration! aberration! I dedicate him to thee, be thou his guide!"

At Kundry's cries the young girls come forth from the palace. Klingsor, armed with the sacred lance, throws himself upon Parsifal, but the divine steel cannot harm him who has remained pure; it rests suspended miraculously above him. The young hero seizes the weapon and traces the sign of the cross in space. At this symbol the magic castle crumbles away and disappears, the garden withers, the young girls, like dying flowers, droop and sink to the earth; nothing is now seen save an arid desert, with mountains and snowy peaks in the distance. Parsifal, striding over the ruins, moves away, uttering a last word of hope to the sinner: "Thou knowest where alone thou wilt see me again."

THIRD ACT.

THE third act takes us back to the domain of the Grail. The spring festival gladdens the forest, everything is in flower, the tender verdure of the fields is sown with Easter flowers, the stream forces itself a passage through clusters of lilies of the valley. It is the day sacred to all, upon which humanity was redeemed,— Good Friday. Gurnemanz, now quite aged, comes forth from an humble hut hidden among the trees. He has heard a groan and a lament, the mournful tone of which is not unknown to him. He approaches the thicket, and raises a woman who appears to be dead. He was not deceived. It is indeed the strange heathen, whom he has already roused from this sleep, so like unto death. Yes, it is Kundry; behold her as she arouses herself, casting about a searching glance which is no longer savage. " To serve, to serve," she murmurs, and she goes off to the side of the cabin, to apply herself to the most humble labors. Gurnemanz, surprised, watches her proceedings, but his attention is soon attracted by a stranger, who advances hesitatingly and dreamily in the refreshing calm of the forest. He is clad in black armor, his helmet is closed, and he holds his lance lowered. Slowly he draws near and seats himself by the spring.

" Greeting, my guest," says Gurnemanz: "Dost thou not know what day this is? Quickly lay aside thy arms; offend not the Saviour, who, stripped of all defense, on this day offered his divine blood for the salvation of the world." The sombre knight obeys; he takes off his helmet and loosens his armor. Gurnemanz then recognizes Parsifal, the harmless fool, whom he had sent away so roughly. With deep emotion he imagines that he recognizes also the sacred lance, long before carried away from the sanctuary. The young man, who looks calmly about him, recognizes Gurnemanz, and extends his hand to him. "I am happy to have found thee again,"-he says.

"What, thou knowest me yet? dost thou remember him, whom grief and distress have bent so low? How camest thou here, and from what place?"

"I am come in the paths of error and suffering," replies Parsifal. "Can I believe myself delivered, since once again I hear the rustling of this forest, and salute thee again, thou good old man?"

"Tell me, to whom should the path which thou seekest lead?"

"To him whose lament I formerly heard in bewildered surprise, to him for

whose salvation I to-day believe myself
to be elected. But alas! a horrible curse
condemns me never to find the road to sal-
vation, and to wander in unknown paths.
When I seemed to have found it, miseries
without number, with struggles and con-
flicts, chased me from the path. Then
had I almost despaired of keeping the
sacred arm in safety. In the effort to pre-
serve and defend it I received wounds
from every side, for I could not make use
of it in the combat. Inviolate I kept it
by my side. I take it back again, it glitters
there, august and radiant, the Grail's holy
lance'!"

"Oh mercy! supreme blessing! Holy
and most august miracle!" exclaims the old
man, with enthusiasm; "if it be a maledic-
tion that turned thee from the true path,
believe me, my lord, it has yielded, for
thou art in the domain of the Grail, and
its knighthood awaits thee. Ah! it stands
in sore need of the salvation which thou

bringest! Since the day that thou wert
here, mourning and anguish have aug-
mented even to supreme distress. Am-
fortas, revolting against his wound, in
sullen obstinacy, longed for death ;
neither the supplications nor the grief of
his knights could impel him to fulfil his holy
office. For a long time the Grail has re-
mained enclosed in its shrine, and its con-
trite guardian, who could not die, should
he contemplate it, hopes thus to enforce
his end, and terminate with his life his
torment. The sacred nourishment is
denied us; also, our heroic strength per-
ishes. Messages and distant calls to holy
combats no longer reach us. The knight-
hood, deprived of chief and courage, wan-
ders miserable and wan. Here in the
corner of the forest I have hidden myself
in solitude, tranquilly awaiting death,
which has already become the lot of my
old lord of arms, Titurel; for the sainted
hero, being no longer revived by the

sight of the Grail, died a man like all others.

"And it is I who caused all this misery!" cries Parsifal, with a burst of grief. "Ah! what sin, what a mass of misdeeds must have weighed upon this fool's head from eternity, inasmuch as, chosen for the redemption, after having wandered distractedly, I see the last path to salvation vanish." He sinks swooning upon a grassy hillock. Gurnemanz supports him, and aided by Kundry endeavors to revive him. Like a new Jordan, the limpid stream will refresh his brow and efface the sin; it will wash the dust of long wandering and journeys from his weary feet. Kundry, like Magdalen, passionately repentant, will shed perfumes upon these feet, and will wipe them in her silken flowing hair, and Gurnemanz, understanding that the day of salvation has come at last, and that the Grail has a new king, will pour the sacred oil upon Parsifal's head.

"Thus I bless thee, and consecrate thee king, thou innocent, compassionate martyr, thou doer of holy deeds! Inasmuch as thou hast suffered all the sufferings of the redeemed, be this last burden taken from thy brow." And the first act of the new king is to pour the baptismal water upon the head of the prostrate and weeping sinner, Kundry.

"Thy tears are become a holy dew," he says to her with divine tenderness, "thou weepest! See, Nature rejoices!" and he kisses her upon the forehead.

The swelling sound of bells in the distance announces Titurel's funeral. As in the first act, the country is gradually transformed, and soon long files of knights in mourning are seen in the galleries escorting the remains of Titurel. Finally the temple reappears, and the knights who carry the Grail and the litter upon which Amfortas is stretched meet the funeral procession.

"Whom does this casket that you bear
in sorrow enclose?" they say, "while we
attend the shrine which shields the Grail."

"This casket encloses the sainted hero
to whom God confided himself; we bear
Titurel."

"What has struck down him whom
even God protected?"

"It was the heavy burden of age that
hastened his end, as he saw the Grail no
more."   •

"Who prevented him from beholding
the Grail and its blessings?"

"He whom you attend, the guilty
guardian."

"We escort him once more to-day, be-
cause for the last time he wills to dis-
charge his priesthood."

"Woe, woe! for the last time be re-
called to the duties of thy office!"

But Amfortas, distracted with grief,
raises himself upon his couch. "Yes,
woe!" he cries, "woe to me! My father!

hero thrice blessed, toward whom the angels bent; I who coveted death; it is thy death I have caused. Oh, thou who now beholdest, in divine light, the Redeemer himself, implore him that he may grant me death at last! Death! death! only grace! May the terrible wound and venom cease, — the wasted heat grow cold! I invoke thee, my father, cry to him: Saviour, grant peace to my son."

"Uncover the tabernacle," cry the knights, pressing in disorder about Amfortas; "fulfil thy priestly office; thy father commands thee; thou must, thou must!"

But the wretched man, in a frenzy of despair, throws himself into the midst of them, tearing his garments. "No, no! never more! Ah! I already feel the shadow of death upon me, and must I return once again to life? Which of you would force me to live since you can give me nothing but death? Behold, the wound yawns, see the poison and my blood! Steep your swords in my wound even to the hilt! Rise, heroes! Destroy with one blow the sinner and his torment; and the Grail will then shine brightly for you by its own virtue!"

All have drawn back in terror. Parsifal then advances solemnly; stretches forth the divine lance, and with its point touches the side of Amfortas. "One arm only is propitious," he says; "the lance that opened the wound can alone close it. Be healed, redeemed, and saved! May thy suffering, which gave supreme strength to compassion, and the power of the purest wisdom to the timorous brother, be sanctified! I restore to you the sacred lance!"

And while Amfortas and Gurnemanz kneel to do him homage, and Kundry, delivered at last, dies at his feet with a look of gratitude, Parsifal ascends toward the altar, and raises for the first time the Grail in all its splendor above the heads of the enraptured knights.

"Miracle of supreme blessing! redemption to the redeemer!"

And voices which seem celestial, sound from the dome's very heights.